RISK, HEALTH AND WELFARE

RISK, HEALTH AND WELFARE
Policies, strategies and practice

Edited by
Andy Alaszewski, Larry Harrison and Jill Manthorpe

Open University Press
Buckingham • Philadelphia

Open University Press
Celtic Court
22 Ballmoor
Buckingham
MK18 1XW

email: enquiries@openup.co.uk
world wide web: http://www.openup.co.uk

and
325 Chestnut Street
Philadelphia, PA 19106, USA

First Published 1998

A catalogue record of this book is available from the British Library

ISBN   0 335 19870 8 (hb)   0 335 19869 4 (pb)

Library of Congress Cataloging-in-Publication Data
Risk, health, and welfare : policies, strategies, and practice / Andy Alaszewski,
    Larry Harrison and Jill Manthorpe (editors).
      p.   cm.
    Includes bibliographical references and index.
    ISBN 0-335-19870-8 (hardcover). – ISBN 0-335-19869-4 (pbk.)
    1. Public welfare – Great Britain.   2. Public health – Great Britain.
  3. Risk.   4. Great Britain–Social Policy.   5. Medical policy – Great Britain.
  I. Alaszewski, Andy.   II. Harrison, Larry, 1946–   .   III. Manthorpe, Jill, 1955–   .
  HV248.R54   1998
  361.9412 – dc21   98–14539
                                                                                                CIP

Typeset by Type Study, Scarborough, North Yorkshire
Printed in Great Britain by St Edmundsbury Press Ltd, Bury St Edmunds, Suffolk

CONTENTS

ACKNOWLEDGEMENTS

This book draws on research funded by the Economic and Social Research Council (ESRC) and the English National Board for Nursing, Midwifery and Health Visiting (ENB). We would like to thank both agencies for their support and for permission to draw on the findings of our research. It is important to stress that all the views expressed are those of the authors.

The editors have been involved with the writing of all the chapters in this book. However, since the extent of their involvement varied, only the main contributor(s) to each chapter are explicitly acknowledged as authors. A number of researchers contributed to the ESRC and the ENB projects including Mike Walsh, Linda Tindall and Helen Alaszewski. We would like particularly to acknowledge the contribution of Mike Walsh, especially in collecting the data which informs Chapters 3 and 4. His appointment to a lectureship in the School of Nursing at the University of Hull meant he was unable to play an active role in writing this book.

Chapter 3 uses material published in *Health and Social Care in the Community* (Alaszewski and Manthorpe 1998) and we thank the publishers of this journal, Blackwells, for permission to use the material.

PREFACE

In health and welfare services there are fads and fashions. In the 1970s, social workers and health workers were encouraged to identify and meet service users' needs; in the 1980s they were expected to provide quality services to consumers or customers; and in the 1990s they are expected to protect users, themselves and the public from risk, danger and harm. Modern society has been named a 'risk society' (Beck 1992) in which welfare systems play a key role by regulating and managing personal and collective risks (Giddens 1994).

The School of Community and Health Studies first became involved in research issues through the work of its Institute of Health Studies in the 1980s. The Department of Health commissioned the Institute to undertake an evaluative study of a community-based unit for children who had a profound learning disability. The voluntary agency establishing the unit, Barnardo's, had a strong commitment to enabling the children to experience ordinary living and the risks associated with it. However, it was clear that there were problems in achieving this desirable objective. The children had serious difficulties communicating so it was problematic to identify what they enjoyed and to enable them to make choices. Some of the children were 'medically fragile', so the care staff and unit managers had to balance safety and choice. For example, the unit was the children's home but it was also the staff's place of work so there was tension between creating a homely environment and a safe place of work. The unit was located in a new residential area so there was a dilemma related to the neighbours; should they be provided with information before the children moved in, would it allay or create fears and anxieties? From the perspective of the late 1990s, it is clear that all these issues were related to risk assessment and management, but at the time, this was not so obvious (see Alaszewski and Ong 1990; Alaszewski and Dodson 1991).

In this book we explore the relevance of risk for the development of health and welfare services, especially for vulnerable people living in the community. Although it draws on research we have conducted in the 1990s, the book is not a research monograph. We see it as an exploration of the key issues informed by some of the insights and information generated by our research and as a text that will inform the development of agencies' policies and professional practice.

The book is divided into four parts. In Part 1 we examine the context of risk assessment and management in contemporary systems of health and welfare. In Chapter 1, we examine the alternative ways in which risk can be defined, consider the 'iceberg' of risk related concepts and explore why modern society is increasingly seen as a 'risk society'. In Chapter 2, we consider how risk has influenced the development of national policy for vulnerable and/or dangerous people.

In Part 2, we consider the ways in which health and welfare agencies seek to manage risk. In Chapter 3, we examine the formal structures and processes of risk management in health and welfare organizations. We re-examine classic literature from a risk perspective highlighting the strategic choices which agencies can and do make. In Chapter 4, we consider the limitations of the formal approach and examine how informal relations shape agency risk management strategies.

In Part 3, we focus on the impact of front-line workers, especially health and welfare professionals, on the management of risk. In Chapter 5, we review the factors which shape professional practice, especially different patterns of accountability and control. Agencies and their policies are clearly important but other aspects such as professional and legal accountability need to be considered. In Chapter 6, we explore the reality of professional practice by examining professional perceptions of risk and the types of decisions they make.

Part 4 is the conclusion. This sets the insights and findings of the book within a broader conceptual context. It examines the limitations of current conceptual foundations of health and welfare services and shows how these limitations may be overcome and professional practice liberated through the imaginative and creative use of risk.

Andy Alaszewski, Larry Harrison and Jill Manthorpe

Part 1

DEFINITIONS AND POLICIES: SETTING THE SCENE

RISK IN MODERN SOCIETY

Andy Alaszewski

This chapter provides the context for our analysis of risk and social welfare. In the first section, we examine how risk is defined and used both in everyday communication and in the specialist literature. In the second section, we develop our discussion identifying an 'iceberg' of risk-related concepts which underpin the different ways in which the concept of risk is used. Finally, we move on to explore the importance of risk in late modern society.

DEFINING AND USING THE CONCEPT OF RISK

Everyday usage

Current usage
'Risk' is an important word in contemporary spoken and written English. It is widely used in commentaries on, or explanation of, current affairs. For example, an edition of the daily newspaper, *The Independent*, chosen at random, contained two headlines using the word 'risk':

Public workers' rights at risk

Doctor in aids scare struck off for ignoring risk
(*The Independent*, 12 March 1997)

In popular usage risk indicates a threat or a danger to an individual or a group of individuals. This is clear in the various dictionary definitions of risk. For example, the *Oxford English Dictionary*'s first definition of risk is:

Hazard, danger; exposure to mischance or peril.
(1989: 987)

and the *Chambers English Dictionary* includes the following definitions:

hazard, danger, chance of loss or injury, the degree of probability of loss: a person, thing, or factor likely to cause loss or danger. vb to expose to hazard: to incur the chance of unfortunate consequences by [doing something].

(1990: 1268)

This everyday usage tends to be incorporated into some expert literature, especially when the meaning of risk is treated as self-evident and unproblematic. For example, Dobos in a study of nurses' perspectives of risk defined risk as:

any situation in which the outcome is uncertain and in which something of value could be lost.

(Dobos 1992: 1304)

Background to the term
The word 'risk' appears to have entered the English language in the seventeenth century from the French *risque*, derived from the Italian *risco*. Ayto suggested that this is a derivative of the Italian verb *riscare*, meaning to 'run into danger' (1990: 446). The development of the original Italian word is obscure. Wharton (1992) traced the origins of 'risk' back to the Arabic *risq* and Latin *risicum*. He argued that the Arabic word indicated a favourable outcome which was the result of divine intervention. This Arabic word appears to have been absorbed into Greek in the twelfth century, stripped of its religious connotation and used to indicate chance outcomes in general which could have either positive or negative outcomes (Wharton 1992: 4). In Latin, the development of the word is difficult to trace but there is support for the view that it originally had a nautical association and was used to indicate an action which gained an advantage by taking a chance, for example by sailing dangerously close to rocks to shorten a voyage (Ayto 1990: 446).

When 'risk' entered the English language, it was used as both a noun and a verb. As a noun it indicated both chance and consequences, but especially negative consequences. For example, Blount, in his glossography published in 1661 listed 'peril, jeopardy, danger, hazard, and chance' as synonyms for *risque*, (*Oxford English Dictionary* 1989: 987). Vanbrugh in his play *Relapse*, first performed in 1708, used the word in the following way:

To cut my Elder Brother's Throat without the Risque of being hang'd for him.

(cited in *Oxford English Dictionary* 1989: 987)

Dr Johnson, in his dictionary first published in 1755, also emphasized the negative aspects of risk, defining it as 'hazard, danger, chance of harm'. However, among the quotations with which he illustrated contemporary usage of the word was one that had a different emphasis and indicated that risk was also used to mean the chance or possibility of loss balanced against potential gain:

Some run the risk of an absolute ruin for the gaining of a present supply.

(cited in *Oxford English Dictionary* 1989: 988)

As a verb, 'risk' was used to indicate actions which exposed an individual to the chance of injury or loss. Again Johnson's dictionary included a definition that indicates a balancing of gain with loss:

To risque the certainty of little for the chance of much.

(cited in *Oxford English Dictionary* 1989: 988)

However, the Duke of Buckingham's use of 'risk' in 1775 to indicate potential loss appears to have been more common:

Lately the King risqu'd both his kingdoms for offering to imprison Philander.

(cited in *Oxford English Dictionary* 1989: 988)

By the nineteenth century, 'risk' was also being used as an adjective with a strong emphasis on negative consequences. A risky action was one in which there was a high probability of a negative outcome. For example, Cooper in *The Prairie* published in 1827 used risk in the following way:

'Twill be a risky job, and one of small profit!

(cited in *Oxford English Dictionary* 1989: 988)

Comment
In contemporary everyday English the word 'risk' indicates the possibility of unintended and negative consequences of decisions or actions. This combination of probability and consequence has been implicit in the word since it entered the English language in the seventeenth century, with the main emphasis on negative outcomes – although it is also possible to identify some usage in which positive and negative outcomes are compared or balanced.

Specialist usage

In scientific or technical literature, the word 'risk' is used in a number of different ways as different scientific disciplines emphasize and study different aspects of risk. We discuss the specialist usage in:

- epidemiology in which the main emphasis is on identifying and measuring the negative consequences of events;
- statistics in which the emphasis is on measuring and predicting the probability or chance of specific events;
- engineering and operational research in which the chief emphasis is on the relationship between positive and negative consequences of events;
- social science in which most emphasis is on studying the ways that individuals and groups identify and respond to risk.

Epidemiologists define risk as 'the probability that a particular adverse event occurs during a stated period of time, or results from a particular challenge' (Royal Society Study Group 1992: 2). Thus they explore the level of risk associated with different types of disease. This approach may also be used to measure the risks associated with either natural events, such as earthquakes, or systems designed and built by humans such as bridges or computer systems.

In this framework the main concern is with the conditions that are associated with different patterns of adverse events or harm. As the Royal Society Study Group on risk pointed out:

> All risks are conditional, although often the conditions are implied by context rather than explicitly stated. The risk of death while hang-gliding during a seven-day period is small for a randomly selected inhabitant of the UK, but its value will alter substantially according to age, season, weather and membership of a hang-gliding club.
>
> (Royal Society Study Group 1992: 3)

There are a number of ways of exploring the conditions which influence the pattern of health risks. For example, it is possible to study different types of population and the harms they experience or alternatively to examine how different types of activities within populations relate to different levels of harm. The measurement of risk has been particularly well developed in relationship to one type of human activity, cigarette smoking, by the Cancer Studies Unit at the University of Oxford. For example, Doll and Peto's long-term prospective study of all doctors registered and working in the UK begun in 1951 identified the association between smoking and lung cancer (Doll *et al.* 1994).

In *statistics* the focus of study is not so much on nature of the consequences of actions or decisions but on the issues of probability and how information on past outcomes can be used to predict future outcomes. Thus the prime emphasis is on expressing probability of future events in numeric form. Indeed, Bernstein who has written a history of the development of this aspect of risk equates risks with numbers:

> The modern conception of risk is rooted in the Hindu-Arabic numbering system that reached the west seven to eight hundred years ago.
>
> (Bernstein 1996: 3)

The modern mathematical study of risk started at the same time as the word risk was entering the English language. In 1654, a French aristocrat who was interested in both gambling and mathematics challenged the mathematician Pascal to find a way of fairly distributing the stakes of an unfinished game of chance between two players when one of them was ahead. Pascal together with another mathematician, Fermat, solved the problem. In doing so they established the theory of probability which forms the mathematical basis for the study of risk as chance. Using probability theory it is possible to employ existing numerical information to improve the prediction of risk and these predictions can be used to improve the quality of decisions (Bernstein, 1996: 3).

During the following century a series of mathematical insights enabled probability theory to be applied to a range of practical situations in which information about the current and future state of affairs could be expressed numerically, such as the changing price of stocks in the stock markets. For example, Bayes' 'Essay Towards Solving a Problem in the Doctrine of Chances' published posthumously in 1764 examined the ways in which new information modified estimates of probability based on existing information

(Bernstein 1996: 131). His analysis can also be applied to the reverse situation, i.e. the use of existing information on probability to interpret new information, as it has considerable practical application. It provides the basis for interpreting the results of specific diagnostic investigation, for example assessing the odds that a given positive diagnostic test result is, in fact, negative. (For a discussion of the application of Bayes' Theorem to child protection see Alaszewski and Walsh 1995.)

The developments of the new technologies is associated with the development of expertise, especially in *engineering and operational research*. Given the possibility of accidents and failures with potential high consequences, engineers have been concerned to identify and prevent failure. Engineers are concerned with the practical solutions to practical problems. If they operated with perfect knowledge and with infinite resources, they would be able to design totally safe systems in which there was no possibility of failure. However, given the limitation of information and other resources, most designs involve a compromise or trade-off between safety and design objectives. Thus engineers and organizations responsible for regulating their activities are concerned to identify tolerable or 'acceptable' levels of risk, i.e. the point at which the probability of harm is so low that it will be accepted by the public or by insurers as a reasonable risk.

This approach has led to analyses of various man-made hazards using estimates of the likely consequences of potential accidents plus information on the death rates associated with actual accidents, to plot graphs of frequency of incidents against the magnitude of the consequences. Crossland (1992) cited a number of examples of such graphs, including the following example:

> In the Health and Safety Commission Report . . . on Major Hazard Aspects of Transport of Dangerous Materials . . . two lines on the Fn [frequency v number of fatalities] graph are used to define the limits of what are deemed an intolerable societal risk . . . The upper line is based on a risk of 2 in 1000 per year of an accident with 500 deaths [local tolerability line] which for the Canvey Island complex was deemed to be just tolerable, whereas the lower line is set three orders of magnitude lower [negligible line]. A third line, referred to as a local-scrutiny line, is assessed for the particular locality associated with road, rail and marine transport risks. Risk assessments that fall between the top two lines are considered as possibly unjustifiable risks, whereas risks that fall between the lower lines are subject to the 'as low as reasonably practicable' (ALARP) principle.
>
> (Crossland 1992: 26–7)

As an aid for decision making some 'frequency versus number of fatalities' graphs quantify fatalities in financial terms so that the potential harmful consequences can be weighed against the likely benefits in a cost/benefit analysis. This information can then be used as part of a decision-making process.

This approach to risk involves a process of balancing the potential benefits of a decision or course of action against the possible harmful consequences. It has developed in an area of management studies closely associated with engineering and project management, operational research. Wharton working within this tradition offered the following definition of risk: 'A risk is an unintended or unexpected outcome of a decision or course of action' (Wharton 1992: 2).

One of the most important developments in system-failure analysis is the application of various forms of logic diagrams which represent the sequence of failures that occur in a complex system. Of the several types of logic diagram that have been used, those known as event trees and fault trees are now the most widely used:

> An event tree specifies a range of possible outcomes, so that for a given frequency of occurrence of an initiating event, the frequency of a particular outcome is given by the product of the initial frequency with all the probabilities at each of the intervening steps. Such a chain is referred to as an accident sequence . . . A fault tree attempts the reverse process, working back from a particular event (known as the top event) through all the chains of events that are the precursors of the top event. The key components of a fault tree are thus event specifications and logic gates ('and/ or' gates). The engineering application of fault trees dates back to the 1960s in the aerospace industry (Boeing Company 1965) . . . and logic trees are widely used outside engineering, for example in business decision trees.
>
> (Crossland 1992: 16-17)

Approaches used in engineering and operational research tend to treat risk as an objective phenomenon that can be measured. In *social sciences and cultural theory*, risk is often treated as problematic. Different groups identify different types of threat to their safety and security so risk is socially constructed. For example, Douglas reported on lay responses to health risks in a study of perceptions and responses to HIV in Brittany. She argued that professional models and information had little impact on some members of the community:

> The most baffling thing about the pattern is that a large number of the community at risk are impervious to information; either they know unshakeably that they themselves are immune, or recognizing that death is normal they draw the conclusion that to live trying to avoid it is abhorrent.
>
> (Douglas 1992: 111)

Douglas argued that perception of and responses to risk are related to an individual's position in a cultural system. She used the following example to illustrate the ways such an approach enables us to understand responses to health risks:

> A homosexual may be advised by the doctor to give up certain practices because of the danger of AIDS, he may be warned that he is risking his life by retaining these practices. If he replies that he has never been a cautious person, and that the high-risk way of life is what he prefers, he is deploying information about himself to support his claim to be left alone, to do as he likes, to be free of well-wishers' interference. A refusal

to take sound hygienic advice is not attributed to weakness of understanding. It is a preference. To account for preferences there is only cultural theory.

(Douglas 1992: 103)

This preference for a high-risk way of life can be seen in certain occupations and lifestyles, such as mountain climbing or motor racing. Chris Bonnington, one of Britain's most famous mountain climbers, described his attraction to mountain climbing in terms of 'the thrill of risk' (BBC Radio 4, 22 October 1994). Damon Hill, a Formula One Grand Prix driver, when asked about the death of his team mate Ayrton Senna, replied:

I think every driver thought of that . . . It's not something I really want to dwell on, but it made every driver consider whether they really wanted to do this. But you think to yourself, well, that's what I planned to do with my life, and it's what I love doing . . . I love to do something exciting. If there's no risk, there's no life.

(interview with R. Williams, *Independent on Sunday*, 25 September 1994, Sport: 3)

Douglas argued that an individual's cultural bias reflects his or her degree of social integration (group) and the ways in which he or she relates to dominant cultural norms and values (grid). Using a grid/group framework, she developed a typology based on these factors and argues that individuals in different categories will have different perceptions of risk and will utilize different sources to explain and respond to ill health. Her four types were:

- individuals who are members of the central dominant culture who will tend to emphasize the importance of accepting professional advice;
- individuals who are members of a dissenting minority who will be sceptical of established professional advice and may develop strong group loyalties to alternative practitioners;
- individualists or cultural frontiersmen who will tend to be high risk-takers and interested in the latest whizzkid practitioners and
- eccentric isolates who will tend to be fatalists and therefore seek no expert advice.

(Douglas 1992: 104–11)

Thus for Douglas there are no fixed objective measures of risk as each individual and each society will define risk in a different way. She is interested in how and why such social constructions vary.

Comment

Like many concepts used in everyday language and in more technical settings, 'risk' has a variety of different meanings and can be used in different ways. Within the various definitions it is possible to identify two key elements, chance and consequences. Warner, in the Royal Society Risk Study Group Report, offered the following technical specification of risk:

1 *Concept*   A general concept of risk is the chance, in quantitative terms, of a defined hazard occurring. It therefore combines a probabilistic

measure of the occurrence of the primary event(s) with a measure of the consequences of that/those event(s).

2 *Terms*   Risk: a combination of the probability, or frequency, of occurrence of a defined hazard and the magnitude of the consequences of the occurrence.

(Warner 1992: 4).

However, risk is used in different ways. It is possible to identify a narrow common sense definition of risk in which risk is equated with danger and the negative outcomes of events. It is also possible to identify broader definitions in which negative consequences are balanced against positive outcome.

As with many of the key words in contemporary analyses and debates about health and welfare, the ambiguity of the term 'risk' may actually be part of its attractiveness. This ambiguity can be used to disguise potentially threatening issues. For example describing certain children as 'at risk' can conceal the fact that not only are such children in danger of abuse by those responsible for their care but they have most probably already suffered considerable harm from which they have not been protected.

THE RISK ICEBERG

Risk forms the tip of an iceberg of related words and terms. Some of these words tend to amplify the restricted meaning of risk in terms of the negative consequences of events; for example, hazard or harm. Other terms are linked to specific aspects of risk and tend to take the form of risk plus a qualifying term, relating to either a more specialist or technical use, such as risk assessment, or to an everyday use, such as risk taking (see Figure 1.1).

Related concepts

Hazard or danger
Underlying the concept of risk is hazard or danger. A hazard or a danger can be defined as a potential threat which can result in harm, loss, or negative consequences for an individual or group. Thus Warner defined hazard in the following way:

1 *Concept*   A general concept of hazard as applied, for example, to an industrial process, or a commercial organization, is the potential for adverse consequences of some primary event, sequence of events or combination of circumstances.

2 *Terms* Hazard: a situation that could occur during the lifetime of a product, system or plant that has the potential for human injury, damage to property, damage to the environment, or economic loss.

(Warner 1992: 4)

Figure 1.1   The risk iceberg

Harm
Given the emphasis on negative consequences, risk is linked to the concept of
harm, which can be defined as the loss experienced by individuals or groups as
the result of specific events or actions. This concept is crucial in the epidemiological approach to risk which is concerned with the level of harm experienced
by specific populations and the 'risk factors' which increase the probability of
this harm occurring. This often leads to interventions based on the identification of 'risk factors' and 'health promotion' strategies.

For example, epidemiological research has established clear links between
lung cancer and tobacco smoking. The 1992 Government White Paper, *Health
of the Nation* identified the risks of smoking in the following way:

> Smoking has been shown to contribute to approximately 30% of all cancer
> deaths and is responsible for at least 80% of those from lung cancer.
>   (Department of Health 1992: 65)

As the consumption of such smoke is related to a specific human behaviour,
tobacco and especially cigarette smoking, engineering a change in this specific
behaviour will result in health gains. This approach can be seen in the Department of Health's strategy for enhancing the health of the nation. This strategy
set targets for the reduction of a variety of diseases. The lung cancer target is to
reduce the death rate by 30 per cent for men and by 15 per cent for women
under 75 by the year 2010 using 1990 as the baseline year (Department of
Health 1992: 18). The major mechanism for achieving these targets is the
reduction of smoking. The White Paper aims to reduce the levels of harm by
reducing the incidence of the associated risky behaviour.

Vulnerability and dangerousness
Vulnerability refers to an individual's propensity to experience harm; indeed,
the word derives from the Latin *vulnus* or wound (*Chambers Dictionary* 1990:
1952). The *Chambers Dictionary* provides the following definition of vulnerable:

capable of being physically or emotionally wounded or injured; open to successful attack; capable of being persuaded or tempted.

(1990: 1952)

Dangerousness refers to an individual's propensity to cause harm. This meaning is actually implicit in the concept of danger. The *Chambers Dictionary* states that the word derives from the old French *dangier* which referred to the absolute power of a feudal lord and hence the power to hurt (1990: 428). As we will show in our discussion of individual identity in Chapter 2, individuals have at times been seen as both dangerous and vulnerable. Concerns with the threat and uncertainty posed by vulnerable and/or dangerous individuals have been some of the major pressures behind the development of state intervention in social welfare and the development of specific mechanisms for managing such risks since the nineteenth century.

The problems posed by vulnerable and dangerous people indicate the need to develop structures to protect both individuals and society and appropriate mechanisms for managing risks. A former Director of the Health Advisory Service pointed out:

We cannot devolve that responsibility for risk taking down to people who are actually in touch with the clients concerned. We have got to actually make sure that it is a managerially accepted risk. More than that it is an authority risk. You have to have statements from your local council, and from your health authority and maybe even from the government that these risks are okay.

(Horrocks 1989: 30)

Safety refers to the absence of harm and is therefore often used to refer to the processes by which harm is prevented and avoided. Warner discussed safety in the following way:

1 *Concept*   Safety relates to the freedom from risks that are harmful to a person, or group of persons, either local to the hazard, nationally or even worldwide. It is implied that for the consequences of an event to be defined as a hazard, i.e. a potential for causing harm, there is some risk to the human population and therefore safety could not be guaranteed, even if the risk is accepted when judged against some criterion of acceptability.

2 *Terms*   Safety: the freedom from unacceptable risks of personal harm.

(Warner 1992: 6)

The concern with safety has become a major preoccupation. Governments, especially in advanced industrial democracies have become involved in two aspects of safety, environmental protection designed to reduce harm to the general population and health and safety designed to reduce harm to employees. Hood *et al.* (1992) drew attention to the growth of legal regulation in Britain from both UK and European Union legislation:

Compared with the relatively small direct public spending on health, safety and environmental programmes, regulation is perhaps the most visible aspect of public risk management, and one that affects much larger resource commitments through the costs of regulatory compliance. Powers of command, permission, prohibition and penalty are exercised in the UK in the forms of EC directives and regulations, primary and subordinate legislation at national-governmental level and the regulatory decisions of local and other public authorities.

(Hood *et al*. 1992: 146)

Blame and accountability

Blame is the process of allocating responsibility and punishments when accidents occur, i.e. when hazards have not been effectively identified and harm occurs. The *Concise Oxford Dictionary* provides the following definition of blame:

(noun) Censure; responsibility for bad result.

(1964: 122)

Thus allocating blame is part of the process of accountability, identifying who is likely to be blamed if things go wrong and allocating responsibility and blame when things do go wrong. In the health and welfare sector, individuals who are accountable for service users, have a 'duty of care' for them.

Douglas, using a cultural theory approach, argued that the process of allocating blame is central to the process of identifying risk and that blaming is a key social process which performs important social functions. Indeed, the ways in which blame is allocated can be used as a way of classifying social groupings. She notes that:

blaming the victim is a strategy that works in one kind of context, and blaming the outside enemy, a strategy that works in another. Victim blaming facilitates internal social control; outsider blaming enhances loyalty. Both ploys would serve an intention to prevent the community from being riven by dissension. Members committed to a society founded on principles of open adversarial confrontation would not be likely to give credence to either of these stock responses to disaster. The accumulation of instances cited only shows that the incidence of misfortune is likely to be put to political uses.

(Douglas 1986: 59)

Comment

The risk iceberg is partially made up of an interrelated set of words that are linked around issues of chance and outcome. There is a degree of interchangeability between these words and a degree of circularity in their definitions. For example the main definition of danger in the Chambers' definition is 'peril, hazard or risk' (Chambers 1990: 1952) while both the *Oxford English Dictionary* and *Chambers English Dictionary* include hazard and danger within their definition of risk. There are other terms within the iceberg that amplify aspects of risk and indicate different aspects of risk. These approaches include risk assessment, risk analysis, risk management, risk taking and risk perception and it is to these we turn next.

Qualifying terms

Risk assessment and risk analysis

Risk assessment and risk analysis are linked to hazard; indeed, they might more accurately be referred to as hazard assessment or hazard analysis. These approaches are often concerned with identifying actual and potential accidents and disasters.

Risk assessment is concerned with identifying the hazards which can cause an accident or disaster whereas risk analysis is also concerned with the factors that result in accidents or disasters. This approach can be seen in the work of Turner who has examined a number of major accidents which he saw as 'very complex, unintended events' (Turner 1992: 2). Analysing these events, he found that they shared common features. For example, prior to the major accident there is usually an 'incubation' period during which there are warning signals, such as near misses or minor accidents. Key groups, such as senior managers, have developed rigid belief systems which lead them to disregard these warnings (Turner 1992: p. 8).

Although they do not explicitly use the concepts of risk analysis, public investigations into accidents are in practice case studies in risk analysis. These investigations have played an important part in developing systems in enterprises which have a major impact on the public, such as public transport systems. Each major rail, shipping and air disaster is followed by an investigation and a public inquiry to identify causes and to improve safety systems. They may also allocate blame or lead to legal actions as in the Zeebrugge car ferry disaster in March 1987.

This approach to risk is also evident in the health and welfare area; indeed, the development of various aspects of government policy such as mental health legislation can be traced back to scandals and inquiries at the beginning of the nineteenth century (see Jones 1972 and Fennell 1995). In the mid-twentieth century the expansion of the role of the state in the funding and regulation of health and welfare seemed to create a safe, incident-free system. However, scandals and incidents re-emerged at the end of the 1960s, with inquiries into long-stay hospitals and child abuse cases in social services. During the 1980s, there was a series of high profile inquiries into incidents in child care and mental health which resulted in harm, including death. These inquiries played a major role in identifying and rectifying system failure (see, for example, Hill 1990).

Increasingly, these inquiries have highlighted issues of risk. For example, the child protection inquiries have resulted in legislation (Children Act 1989) which explicitly identified the social workers' role as assessors of the risk of child abuse. Within mental health policy the inquiry into the killing of Jonathan Zito by Christopher Clunis, also highlighted the role of mental health practitioners as risk assessors (Report of the Inquiry into the care and Treatment of Christopher Clunis 1994). The main thrust of the Inquiry Team's recommendations was to develop an effective system for identifying risk, especially when patients who had been detained in hospital under the Mental Health Act (1983) were discharged into the community. Under Section 117 of the Act, Health Authorities and Social Services Authorities already had a duty to provide aftercare for patients who had been detained under Section 3 of the Act. The Inquiry recommended that procedures under Section 117 should be tightened. They recommended that authorities should use a new standard form which would not only record details of agreed aftercare plans but would also include, in the case of patients who had been violent, 'an assessment . . . as to whether the patient's propensity for violence presents any risk to his own health or safety or to the protection of the public' (Report of the Inquiry into the Care and Treatment of Christopher Clunis 1994: para. 45.1.2). In addition, the Inquiry recommended the establishment of a 'nationally based Register for patients subject to S 117 Mental Health Act 1983 Aftercare' (1994: para. 45.2.3) so that, if a discharged patient experienced a relapse, information could be obtained rapidly from his or her hospital records. Both recommendations were, in part, accepted by the government (Department of Health 1996; Stanley and Manthorpe 1997).

Risk communication and risk perception
Risk analysis and assessment leads to a study of how individuals and groups perceive risk and how information about risk is communicated. Not only do the inquiries into accidents and disasters tend to identify human error as a major factor and therefore a failure by individuals and groups to identify and respond to hazards effectively (Turner 1992: 8), but they also attempt to prevent such accidents through regulation. These regulatory regimes are often based on concepts of 'tolerable risk' and, therefore, require some way of assessing how the public view risk in general and tolerable risk in particular. For example, the Inquiry by Sir Frank Layfield into the building of the Sizewell B nuclear plant made the following recommendation in relationship to safety criteria for the plant:

> The opinions of the public should underlie the evaluation of risk. There appears to be no method at present for ascertaining the opinions of the public in such a way that they can be reliably used as the basis for risk evaluation. More research on the subject is needed. As in other complex aspects of public policy where there are benefits and detriments to different groups, Parliament is best placed to represent the public's attitudes to risks.
>
> (Layfield 1987: summary para. 2.101h)

Furthermore, failure to effectively communicate information about risk can have major economic and social consequences. There have been a number of 'food panics', such as 'listeria hysteria' and bovine spongiform encephalopathy (BSE) or mad cow disease, in which government ministers, food producers and some experts have argued that risks of consuming particular foods are minimal. However, the general public have been unwilling to accept these assurances and have altered their behaviour with major consequences for both the producers and the government, yet other more 'real' risks have been neglected. Miller and Reilly summarized the situation in the following way:

In the late nineteen eighties a number of high profile 'food scares' received extensive publicity in the British media. These included stories about salmonella in eggs, listeria in cheese and bovine spongiform encephalopathy (BSE or 'mad-cow' disease) in cattle. While these dramatic food panics received widespread publicity, other issues, which are at least as consequential for human health, have received less dramatic coverage . . . why did this apparently cause a dramatic downturn in the buying and eating of eggs, when 'health warnings' about the links between eating eggs, cholesterol levels in the blood and coronary heart disease have not had similar effects?

(Miller and Reilly 1994: 3)

Risk perception and communication focus on the social processes which shape individual and group awareness of risk. As Pidgeon *et al.* (1992) pointed out, these issues are of interest to social scientists who have played a lead role in studying them:

From the perspective of the social sciences, risk perception involves people's beliefs, attitudes, judgements and feelings, as well as the wider social or cultural values and dispositions that people adopt, towards hazards and their benefits.

(Pidgeon *et al.* 1992: 89)

Pidgeon and colleagues considered that two rather different approaches have emerged in the study of risk perception, one emphasizes the objective nature of risk whereas the other focuses on the subjective interpretation of risk.

The 'objective' approach to risk perception examines how individuals or groups over or under estimate different types of risk. This approach is used in psychological studies where individuals are asked to estimate the probability of a range of hazards. Pidgeon cited a study by Lichtenstein *et al.* (1978) in which educated individuals were asked to estimate the annual frequency in the USA of 40 hazards using the annual death rate from motor vehicle accidents as a reference point. The study found that:

respondents tended to overestimate the number of deaths from infrequent causes such as botulism and tornadoes, but to underestimate the deaths from frequent causes such as cancer and diabetes . . . [a secondary pattern in the data was identified] the types of activity whose fatality were judged to be relatively higher . . . were typically vivid, or imaginable causes of death.

(Pidgeon *et al.* 1992: 99)

Whereas the psychometric approach tends to concentrate on the similarities in the ways different individuals perceive different types of risk, cultural theory suggests that the very concept of risk is socially constructed and that different social groups will identify different types of threats and different risks. The cultural theory perspective was summarized by Marris and colleagues in the following way:

Cultural theorists have argued that the psychological approach, by focusing solely on abstract ratings of risks, has failed to focus on the important issues at stake in judgements about risks. More interesting questions would include: who is trusted to manage risk? who gets blamed in the case of mishap? what constitutes fairness, consent, or accountability? (Douglas 1986). Cultural theory consists of two components. The first is a theoretical approach based on the belief that adherence to a certain pattern of social relationships generates a distinctive way of looking at the world, and *vice versa*: that adherence to a certain world view legitimises a corresponding type of social relations.

(Marris, *et al.* 1996: 5–6)

Risk taking and risk management

Risk taking and risk management both focus on responses to risk. Risk taking is concerned primarily with individual decisions about risk, whereas risk management is concerned with collective or group responses.

Risk taking has tended to focus on individual decision making, especially individual decisions to undertake hazardous activities which are linked to high levels of harm. The most obvious example is smoking. Viscusi has undertaken a detailed study of risk taking in relationship to smoking. He points out that not only are smoking risks primarily voluntary but that since the mid 1970s the main approach to managing the risks has been to change individual behaviour through information rather than making the substance safer:

Smoking risks arise from an individual's choice to engage in smoking behaviour . . . The emphasis instead has been on decreasing smoking activity rather than changing the safety properties of the product, whereas the dominant approach in government risk-regulation efforts over the past quarter century has been a technology-oriented focus. This emphasis of the cigarette risk-regulation efforts on altering behaviour and providing information makes smoking the most well-developed case study for analysing the efficacy of this regulatory approach.

(Viscusi 1992: 3)

Within the risk taking framework, hazardous behaviours are treated as forms of rational action. Hazardous behaviours such as smoking are often seen as a product of ignorance or irrationality, inadequate information or failure to use information appropriately. However, if the outcome seems irrational, then it is likely to reflect the inadequacy of the model being used to explain the action rather than defects of the individuals undertaking the actions. Again Viscusi's study of smoking illustrated this approach:

Although fewer people smoke now than did in the past, many continue to smoke even in the presence of these anti-smoking efforts. A common belief is that individuals who smoke are ignorant of smoking's hazards and are incapable of making risky choices in a reliable manner. The evidence to be examined in this book suggests that we should abandon this stylised view. Instead of widespread ignorance of the risks, there is in fact substantial awareness of the potential hazards of smoking, even among smokers. The levels of awareness differ for various components of the risks of cigarettes. These perceptions reflect the influence of a complex mix of informational and cognitive factors.

(Viscusi 1992: 3–4)

Whereas the study of risk taking is concerned with individual behaviour, risk management is concerned with collective responses to risk. As in the study of risk perception and communication, two approaches can be identified, one approach focuses on the nature of the risk and hazard and the other on variations in societal responses, especially organizational responses, to similar risks or hazards.

The 'hazard-oriented' approach concentrates on responses to different types of hazard. As Hood and colleagues pointed out, the 'hazard-oriented' approach tends to fragment into specialist areas based on the technical study of specific types of study:

> Traditionally, academic research in the field has been divided according to the specific types of risk being managed, notably into *natural hazards, technological hazards* and *social hazards. Natural hazards* emanate from the operation of natural or physical environmental systems extraneous to humankind, such as earthquakes or hurricanes, and there is a specialist field of natural hazard research which has tended to employ human ecological perspectives to examine the 'goodness of fit' between human societies and non-human physical processes . . . The term 'environmental hazards' is increasingly coming to replace 'natural hazards', in recognition of the fact that many hazards in the environment are either produced or exacerbated by human activity (e.g. desertification, floods, acidification). *Technological hazards,* such as explosions or collisions, emanate from human-designed technological systems and there is a diverse literature on the causes and management of such hazards which spans the social and natural sciences. *Social hazards* emanate from human behaviour, such as arson or terrorism.

(Hood *et al.* 1992: 135–6)

The 'institutional-oriented' approach explores variation in responses, especially organizational responses, to hazards. Hood and colleagues argued for a broader focus on the ways institutions are designed to manage risk. In particular, they explore the ways risk is institutionally structured and the nature of the choices made by an organization in relationship to risk management (Hood *et al.* 1992: 148). We will return to these issues in Chapter 3 as they form a central theme in the next part of this book.

Comment

The risk iceberg is made up of a set of interconnected words and terms. These are all linked through a central concern with issues of probability and consequence. However, it is possible to identify a difference in emphasis. In one approach words such as risk, hazard and harm are seen as unproblematic, indeed objective categories. The concern is to examine their impact on individuals and groups in different contexts so that they can be managed more effectively. However, in other approaches risk, hazard and harm are seen as socially constructed categories. Different social groups structure their internal and external relations in different ways and these different structures are linked to how they define and manage risk. Having considered the risk iceberg, we will now consider the significance of risk in contemporary society.

RISK AND SOCIETY

The risk society

Beck (1992) argued that the definition and management of risk permeates modern society, indeed he refers to such societies as risk societies. He argues that early modern industrial society was characterized by industrialized production and individuals' life experiences were related to their access to benefits created, especially wealth. However, increasingly industrial production and modernization are generating not only positive benefits such as wealth but also hazards. Thus individuals' life experiences are increasingly related to the extent to which they are exposed to the hazards and risks of modern society. Thus Beck placed risk within a wide social perspective in the following way:

> In the past, the hazards could be traced back to an undersupply of hygienic technology. Today they have their basis in industrial overproduction. The risks and hazards of today . . . are risks of modernization. They are a wholesale product of industrialization . . . Risk may be defined as a systematic way of dealing with hazards and insecurities induced and introduced by modernization itself.
>
> (Beck 1992: 21)

In this new emerging risk society, the emphasis shifts from the ways benefits such as wealth are distributed to the ways in which harm and risk are distributed. This new form of society is based on increased awareness and control of risk is possible.

Beck argued that the established disadvantaged groups, i.e. the poor, will continue to experience the highest level of risk in the emerging risk society. However the hazards generated by the wealthy through industrial production such as pollution will boomerang back on them. Furthermore, in this new emerging risk society, the response to risk can no longer be restricted to changing isolated aspects of individual lifestyles but must be concerned with the overall structuring of lifestyles and the risks generated by the underlying social and productive processes that shape these lifestyles.

Experts and risk

The role of experts in creating, identifying and managing risks is central to risk society. In situations of uncertainty where the risks are high and it is difficult to measure risk, the task of risk assessment and risk management is taken on by experts in risk, usually professionals, who lay people trust to protect them from hazards. However, events such as 'food panics' indicate that citizens do not always trust the experts who try to reassure them.

The problems created by trusting experts are graphically illustrated by the development of one new medical technology, human growth hormone therapy. This therapy was the subject of a 'World in Action' television programme investigation in 1994. The hormone replacement programme began in the early 1960s when scientists and clinicians discovered that if growth hormones extracted from the human pituitary gland were injected into young children this would accelerate their growth so that undersized children could be treated until they caught up with their normal sized peers. Some 2000 children were treated before it became clear that they were in danger of developing Creutzfeldt Jakob Disease, a disease similar to BSE or Mad Cow Disease which results in deterioration of the brain tissue and rapid death. Although concerns were first voiced by experts in the 1970s, the hormone replacement programme was not terminated until 1985 and the Department of Health did not set up a counselling service for individuals who had received human growth hormone treatment until May 1992, by which time the first victims had already died. The official view is that this was an unavoidable accident. The patients and their parents felt they were deprived of information about the potential risks and had therefore never been able to make an informed choice or decision. Their trust in experts was misplaced.

Clearly new health technologies carry a risk. While Beck takes a negative view of both technology and the experts who foster its development, it is possible to develop a more positive response. Giddens argues that the development of technology changes the pattern of risk from high probability and low consequence to low probability and high consequence. Thus while there is 'a reduction in life-threatening risks for the individual' (1990: 114), there is also 'a globalisation of high-consequence risk' (1990: 114). These are disasters which may affect the whole planet such as a nuclear accident or global warming. As Giddens pointed out, whether we like it or not: 'To live in the universe of high modernity is to live in an environment of chance and risk, the inevitable concomitants of a system geared to the domination of nature' (Giddens 1990: 109).

Trust and risk

Giddens saw risk as a central feature of modern society, but it is important to note that he used the word risk solely in terms of negative consequences, i.e. threats to individual and collective well-being and security. He contrasted it to trust which he saw as a way of providing individuals and groups with security and counteracting the threats posed by risk.

Giddens argued that modernity does not create risk and trust; it changes their nature (Giddens 1990: 100–11). Premodern societies tend to be highly localized in terms of their social, political and economic relations. Thus risk and trust are also localized and personalized with strong emphasis on personal relations of trust to protect the individual. Modernization disrupts these highly personalized and localized relations. The development of rapid methods of communication and transport such as satellite TV and telephone and air

Diagram 1.1: Environments of trust and risk in pre-modern and modern cultures

PRE-MODERN *General context:* **overriding importance of localized trust**	MODERN *General context:* **trust relations vested in disembedded abstract systems**
Environment of trust	**Environment of trust**
1 *Kinship relations* – as an organizing device for stabilizing social ties across time-space	1 *Personal relationships* – or sexual intimacy as means of stabilizing social ties
2 *The local community* – as a *place*, providing a familiar milieu	2 *Abstract systems* – as a means of stabilizing relations across indefinite spans of time-space
3 *Religious cosmologies* – as modes of belief and ritual practice providing a providential interpretation of human life and of nature	3 *Future-oriented* – counter-factual thought as a mode of connecting past and present
4 *Tradition* – as a means of connecting present and future; past-oriented in reversible time.	
Environment of risk	**Environment of risk**
1 Threats and dangers emanating from *nature,* such as the prevalence of infectious diseases, climatic unreliability, floods, or other natural disasters	1 Threats and dangers emanating from the *reflexivity* of modernity
2 The threat of *human violence* from marauding armies, local warlords, brigands, or robbers	2 The threat of *human violence* from the industrialization of war
3 Risk of a *fall from religious grace* or of malicious magical influence	3 The threat of *personal meaninglessness* deriving from the reflexivity of modernity as applied to the self

Source: Giddens 1990: 102

travel have resulted in process of globalization. Traditional beliefs and technologies, such as belief in magic and using specialists to identify witches, may continue to exist parallel to modern beliefs and technologies but are marginalized or suppressed, i.e. do not attract the interest, support and resources from dominant social élites and tend to be practised by the poorer or more marginal members of society who do not have access to modern technologies.

Globalization also creates interdependency between social groups living in different countries. This interdependency tends to increase social stability and individual security but shifts trust from personalized systems to highly abstract and impersonal systems. For example, a stable world economic structure based on exchangeable currencies means that groups tend to have more secure economic bases and that individuals can travel relatively more freely and securely between countries, i.e. creates the conditions for mass tourism and migration. However, greater short-term security and stability is also associated with increased vulnerability to world-wide catastrophes. For example, a major increase in the price of oil as occurred in 1973, or a fall in prices in one of the world's major stock markets as occurred in 1989, is likely to influence prices in the other markets and may lead to a general world-wide economic recession and associated social turbulence. Individuals within this global society will tend to experience an individual sense of meaningless. Giddens summarized the changing pattern of trust and risk in a diagram (see Diagram 1.1).

Risk and need

Giddens argued that the concept of risk can be applied to welfare services within contemporary society. Indeed, he suggests that using it can lead to a rethinking of welfare. He argues that all welfare systems are designed to manage individuals' risks but that changes in the nature of risk has resulted in a crisis in these systems. In his view, the British welfare state was established in the 1940s to deal with 'external' risks, 'misfortunes that affect people through no fault of their own' (Giddens 1994: 24). However, increasingly risk is the result of individual's own or other people's actions such as alcohol misuse or divorce. Managing such risks requires the active participation of the affected individuals.

We shall show in the remaining chapters of this book that if risk is used in a creative and systematic way it can contribute to the development of health and welfare services. For example, it would facilitate the identification and management of different forms of risks, such as risks created by the intrinsic vulnerability of some individuals with a learning disability, risks associated with individual behaviours such as drug misuse and risks associated with environmental hazards such as infectious disease.

Comment

It is clear that risk and its management are central features of modern society. Given the complexity of some of the issues and the range of terms involved it is important to provide a clear definition of risk. For the purposes of this study we use a definition derived from social sciences. We define risk as:

> the possibility that a given course of action will not achieve its desired and intended outcome but instead some undesired and undesirable situation will develop.
>
> (adapted from Alaszewski and Manthorpe 1991: 277)

This definition emphasizes three elements:

- the intention of actions, thus risk involves *unintended* consequences;
- the consequences of action;
- the (unspecified) probability that (negative) consequences will occur.

Given the wide variety of ways in which risk is studied, it is also important to specify which area of risk we are interested in. This book focuses on risk management within health and welfare services. Viewed from the perspective of these services, risk involves a threat to the well-being of individuals and groups within society. Risk management examines the different strategies which welfare agencies use to manage this threat.

In the next chapter we will examine the development of 'welfare' policy for two groups of individuals, vulnerable children and adults with a learning disability, to explore the ways in which risks have been and are defined within official policy.

2

RISK AND VULNERABLE PEOPLE: THE DEVELOPMENT OF POLICY

Linda Tindall and Andy Alaszewski

In this chapter we consider national policy in respect of risk and vulnerable people. The aims of the chapter are twofold; first, to examine links between broad social change, developments in policy and changes in the official identity of vulnerable people (as constructed in policy), and secondly to examine the changing perceptions of policy makers with regard to the types of risk posed by, and to, vulnerable people, and the way in which these risks are to be managed.

Our particular concern is with contemporary policy, which establishes the framework in which risk is managed at local level, by agencies and by professionals. But the current national policy framework does not represent a new beginning; it has been fundamentally influenced by what has gone before. We therefore locate contemporary policy within its broad historical context, to highlight the increasing visibility and salience of risk through time, as a social 'problem' requiring a national policy response.

We approached our task by applying content analysis techniques, to key national policy statements and other relevant documents, using the concept of 'risk', and synonyms such as hazard, harm and danger, as the focus of our analysis. We explored the policy framework in England within three broad periods of time: pre-modern (to about 1600), early modern (from 1600 to approximately 1950) and late modern (after 1950).

Any attempt to describe comprehensively policy change across eight centuries would be immediately confounded by the volume of national policy statements which have been produced in respect of vulnerable people, all of which would be potentially relevant. Clearly such an undertaking would be inappropriate in a book such as this as the historical dimension alone would extend to many volumes! To overcome the problem that this 'data overload' presents, we isolate one 'defining moment', within each of the broad time periods, to illustrate prevailing political perceptions regarding vulnerable people and risk. These will be examined in turn, using a consistent structure throughout.

Bearing in mind that policy does not arise in a vacuum, but is shaped by the context in which it is constructed, we start by locating our defining moment within its broad social, economic, technological and political context. We then identify the key policy statements and consider their implications, both for vulnerable people and those with official responsibility for risk management.

It is important to reiterate that this approach should not be confused with a history of policy development; such studies are to be found elsewhere (see, for example, Heywood 1978; Parton 1985 and Fox Harding 1991 in respect of vulnerable children and Jones 1972; Alaszewski 1988 and Race 1995 with regard to people with learning disabilities). Rather we highlight specific official perceptions towards risk and vulnerable people, at *particular* points in time, to demonstrate the way these perceptions have changed, becoming ever more varied as a response to increasingly complex patterns of social living.

In the final section (late modern), we identify the tension which exists in current national policy between competing policy objectives, in particular the unresolved tension between service user empowerment and professional accountability. This tension must be managed by agencies and professionals through the development of local policies and procedures. Thus this chapter provides the background to the issues which are the subject of the rest of this book.

PRE-MODERN POLICY AND VULNERABLE INDIVIDUALS

Context

Although official recognition of risks associated with vulnerable children and adults with learning disabilities can be traced back to Saxon times (see, for example, the laws of Alfred which are concerned with children or other helpless people; Attenborough 1922), it was not until the thirteenth century that the process of law-making was accompanied by contemporary commentaries which amplify the purpose of the laws and therefore provide some insight into the ways that contemporaries conceptualized social problems.

English society at the end of the thirteenth century was characterized by predominantly rural patterns of living, based upon subsistence agriculture. Society was essentially small-scale and, given limitations of communications, based on face-to-face interactions within highly localized communities. The social structure was characterized by the distinctive, hierarchical pattern of social relations known as feudalism.

Bloch has captured the essence of European feudalism in the following way:

> In feudal society the characteristic human bond was the subordinate's link with a nearby chief. From one level to another the ties thus formed – like so many chains branching out indefinitely – joined the smallest to the greatest.
>
> (Bloch 1961: 44)

Underlying this hierarchy was a division between a dominant military élite, the King and the Barons, and a subject peasantry, but at each level in the hierarchy a dual relationship existed – the lord of some was the subordinate of another.

The relationship between lord and subordinate was tight knit and reciprocal, based, traditionally, upon the giving of land, status and protection in return for service. However, it is important to recognize that this description reflects an 'ideal type' which belies the different patterns of feudal relations between different geographical areas, the complex nature of relations within and between each level of the feudal hierarchy and the changing nature of those relations during the feudal period. For example, in England, as early as the late twelfth century, the traditional 'land for service' relationship was already giving way to one increasingly based upon financial transactions with the emergence and subsequent development of a market based economy (Poole 1946).

Within feudal society, relations were primarily based on social status, i.e. an individual's social, economic and political identity were ascribed, usually on the basis of birth and parentage. The importance of ascribed social status, meant that individual importance and value was highly differentiated. Individuals at the top of the social hierarchy were of high interest and value while individuals at the bottom were of no particular interest (unless they became a threat to the established order).

Theoretically, social problems in the modern sense, such as unemployment or destitution due to sickness or old age, could not arise within the feudal structure because of the protective responsibility of liege lords (de Schweinitz 1947). In practice, however:

> the poor, the aged and the impotent, were encumbrances undeserving of care or consideration; and if they could not obtain subsistence by begging or stealing, they were left to starve. Those only were cared for who were able to . . . assist in upholding the power . . . of the feudal baron or head lord, whose influence, and often whose safety, depended on the number and hardihood of his followers.
>
> (Nicholls 1854: 21–2)

In so far as concerns existed during the mediaeval period about the risks of destitution faced by vulnerable people, these were seen to be appropriate to the role of the church and charitable giving rather than for the state (Tierney 1959). Thus it is not surprising that in this period specific official interventions in respect of risk and vulnerable people were largely restricted to the élite.

The mediaeval political system reflected the social structure in which it existed. The role of the monarch was that of feudal overlord, with the responsibilities for protection and service this entailed. The monarch was responsible for protection of the realm but in return had the right to expect obedience from his vassals. In terms of service, the King was the vassal of God. As Warren put it: 'He was the Vicar of God on earth, into whose care and protection the people of his realm were committed, and who owed him a duty of obedience as to the Elect of God' (Warren 1987: 15-16).

As the most powerful families in the land were the King's immediate subordinates this relationship conferred extensive monarchical power (Waugh 1988).

The unique and divine status of the king legitimated a central role for him in decision making but, as Warren (1987) further argued, this did not represent unfettered power, 'divine grace was conferred to do God's will not his own' (p. 16). Furthermore, a traditional expectation remained from pre-feudal times that the king would consult with, and gain the consent of 'the community' or its representatives when taking important decisions, even though he would not necessarily be bound by their views (Mitteis 1975). However, as the king was in a position to choose his closest advisers this gave him substantial control over the activities of government and processes such as law making (Brown 1992).

Throughout the thirteenth century in particular a slow but important change was taking place in the pattern and structures of government, underpinned by intermittent conflict between the king and his barons regarding the appropriate boundaries of the monarch's ultimate power in decision making. As a consequence of these power struggles, and the impossible burden which personal governance imposes upon one person, the role of the monarch's advisers and community representatives became increasingly strengthened and formalized. By the Tudor period, the 'King's Council' of the Plantagenet King Henry III (1216–71) had evolved into the current parliamentary system consisting of Commons and Lords.

The key policy statements

Since government in the thirteenth century was rudimentary by today's standards and record keeping limited, the evidence which survives from this period on policy is sparse and, at times, difficult to interpret. Indeed, contemporaries did not see government processes such as law making as innovatory. Rather they were seen as codification of traditional customs and practices which formed the basis of Common Law. Law makers tended to see their role in terms of codifying such custom and practice and as such did not need to justify the laws. Early statutes lack detail and so offer limited insight into the nature of the society in which they were constructed (Pollock and Maitland 1923). However, there are contemporary commentaries upon the law which do provide additional information. Two such commentaries were written in approximately 1290 – Britton (1865) and Fleta (1984). Thus the late thirteenth century is a defining moment because some understanding can be gained of the thinking behind policy as embodied in laws.

Relevant pre-modern policy statements fall into two main groups, those concerned with the vulnerable élite and those concerned with vulnerable poor people. Statutes of 1225 (Henry III 1225a–d) for example, dealt with issues arising from the inheritance of property and office by children. With regard to adults with learning disabilities (to use modern language) the 'Praerogativa Regis' outlines the king's rights in respect of the lands of 'idiots' (in the language of the time). This statute is conventionally cited as Edward II (1324) Cap IX but its exact date and status as a statute are the subject of uncertainty (see Maitland 1891; Waugh 1988: 100). In contrast to these highly specific official interventions in respect of the vulnerable élite, impoverished vulnerable people were dealt with through the general legislative framework aimed at dealing with the problem of poverty, or rather its consequences, social disorder. This began in Saxon times (Aethelstan c930, cited in Attenborough 1922), was developed in the feudal Statute of Labourers (Edward III 1349) and culminated in the 1601 Act for the Relief of the Poor (Elizabeth I 1601).

Policy and vulnerable people

In the year 1290 children, within the élite at least, were perceived by legislators as different from adults. Their vulnerability was recognized, in the sense that they were seen as unable to take on responsibility for managing their lands and affairs (including marriage). Thus the statutes provided for the appointment of a 'Guardian' to take on this role, with a responsibility to 'safeguard' the 'ward' until he or she reached majority (i.e. the end of his or her twenty-first year) (*Fleta* 1984: ch. 9).

Propertied adults with learning disabilities were also officially perceived as different from other adults and *Fleta* makes clear that they were closely equated with children: 'It is the custom to appoint guardians for the lands and persons of idiots and fools for the whole of their lives, and this has been lawful because of their *inability to rule themselves*, being *adjudged ever to be*, as it were, *below full age*' (*Fleta* 1984: ch. 11, para. 8, our italics).

Thus in the late thirteenth century adults with learning disabilities were seen as 'eternal children' and dealt with accordingly. On the other hand, legislators at this time demonstrated respect for the inheritance rights of adults with learning disabilities; they were not simply disinherited.

Although the word 'risk' is not used in these laws, risk and the management of risk, can be seen as important, if implicit, issues. This is revealed by the harms which legislators were seeking to prevent. For example, in respect of children, the Guardian was required to 'deliver to the Heir . . . all his land . . . at the least as he received it, and that without destruction and waste of his men and his goods' (Henry III 1225b).

The Guardian was also required by statute to arrange a marriage for the child which was not 'disparaging' (i.e. one which would not erode the child's social status) (Henry III 1225d). With regard to 'idiots' the law decreed that their 'necessaries' were to be provided for, and that: 'after the death of such idiots [the king] shall render [their lands] to the right heirs, *so that such idiots shall not be aliene*, nor their heirs shall be disinherited' (Edward II 1324, our italics).

On face value, therefore, the content of these laws demonstrate recognition of the vulnerability of children and adults with learning disabilities. Children are presented as vulnerable to, for example, careless or exploitative management of their property by their Guardian, and as being at risk of losing their social status if married inappropriately. Adults with learning disabilities are presented as vulnerable to personal neglect and disinheritance. However, while there is recognition of dangers *to* vulnerable people the major concern of legislators is with preserving property and property rights, i.e. the threat posed *by* the inheritance of vulnerable people to the long-term social, economic and political status, not only of the individual but also of his or her family. The steps adopted are therefore primarily designed to manage this threat.

In contrast, in 1290, the state showed little specific interest in impoverished vulnerable people, unless they became involved in crime. The major concern was with 'robberies, murthers, burnings and theft' and statutory interventions were aimed at dealing with these problems rather than with the interrelated issues of destitution and vulnerability (see, for example, Edward I 1285a). Although the 'ravishment' or abduction of child wards was prohibited by statute (Henry III 1235), and punishable by imprisonment, the major concern was with compensating the rightful owner of the child's marriage (which carried a monetary value) rather than with the impact of the 'offence' upon the child.

In so far as there was concern at this time for the personal well-being of vulnerable people, this was not perceived as a responsibility of the state but of the church. General responsibility for dealing with 'ill-treatment of wife or children' and other 'sins' was the jurisdiction of the ecclesiastical courts, whose involvement depended upon private complaint. Their role declined sharply after 1490, and particularly with the Reformation, when this was taken over by 'new' courts established by the Crown (Harding 1966). However, it appears that these courts did not retain the ecclesiastical courts' responsibility in respect of abused children. Indeed, later in the pre-modern period we find what we might regard as abusive behaviour towards vulnerable people officially sanctioned in statute, such as the public beating with rods of children aged 12–16 years who ran away from their masters, and the whipping of impotent, i.e. disabled or elderly, beggars who went out of their area or begged without a licence (Henry VIII 1530).

Administration and accountability

Given the rudimentary development of government, the major concern of legislators in the thirteenth century was the creation of administrative systems and the identification of accountable individuals. For vulnerable children with property it was the responsibility of the child's 'Guardian' to administer and preserve the child's inheritance for the duration of his or her minority. The Guardian was allowed to take 'reasonable issues, reasonable customs and reasonable services', but in the event of the Guardian making 'destruction or waste of those things that he hath in custody' he would be liable to lose guardianship status and be made to compensate for his mismanagement (Henry III 1225b).

Similarly, in respect of adults with learning disabilities, when the king assumed custody of their lands and property he gained the right to take any profits, but also responsibility to 'preserve them from any disherison' (*Fleta* 1984: ch. 11, para. 8). In reality, however, day-to-day management of royal wardships was delegated by the Crown to its agents, the escheators and subescheators (Waugh 1988). Escheators and their assistants were subject to the same penalties as Guardians if they committed 'waste or destruction'

(Edward I 1278 and Edward I 1300). Thus mechanisms of accountability were based upon the threat of financial penalties.

In terms of the vulnerable poor, official concern was only activated if they became involved in criminal activity. A major problem, as perceived by the king and his advisers, was the failure of towns and other areas of local administration to accept responsibility for bringing criminals to justice. The response therefore was to make local administrators responsible for taking steps to improve security in their area and to make '[t]he people dwelling in the country . . . answerable for the robberies done, and also the damages' (Edward I 1285b). Here again, the emphasis was upon financial penalties.

Comment

Government in the feudal period, in comparison to later periods, was relatively rudimentary and the main sources which defined the nature of vulnerability and official responses to it were the law and commentaries upon the law. In a hierarchically structured society, the perceived nature of the threat and the state response to it varied according to where the vulnerable person was located in the social hierarchy.

Although there is evidence of the feudal state having some interest in and concern about the welfare and wellbeing of vulnerable members of the élite, its primary concern was with matters of property and inheritance, and the threat posed by vulnerable inheritors to the long-term social, economic and political status of themselves and their families. In terms of individuals at the bottom of the social hierarchy, the concern was with managing generalized, collective threats to social order rather than with the specific, personalized threats faced by impoverished vulnerable people. The relief of poverty and the management of abuse to wives or children was seen as an issue for church not the state.

Given the relatively underdeveloped nature of the machinery of government during this period, the main aim of legislators was to develop administrative systems to manage the different threats posed by vulnerable people. This depended upon where they were situated in the social hierarchy and the identification of individuals who could be held to account for implementing the law. Mechanisms of accountability were therefore focused upon matters of administration rather than ensuring quality of personal care. Accountability was enforced by the threat of financial penalties.

EARLY MODERN POLICY: THE LIBERAL REFORMS

Context

The development of early modern society was characterized by an economic and social transformation, often referred to as the 'industrial revolution'. In England, the origins of these changes can be traced back to the 1500s. The technological and economic changes involved improvements in communication systems, the development of commercial agriculture, the factory system and heavy industry.

Economic changes were associated with social changes and in particular the growth of cities and conurbations. With improvements in communications, new factories and industries were less dependent on supplies of power and raw materials but, as they tended to be labour intensive, they were more dependent on the supply of unskilled and semi-skilled labour. Industrial production tended to concentrate in towns or cities which provided a supply of wage labour, and this concentration in turn sustained urban growth by creating a demand for labour. In the early modern period, England changed from a predominantly rural and agrarian society to a predominantly urban and industrial society.

Overt and visible economic changes such as the expansion of the cities were underpinned by less visible changes in the pattern of social relations associated with the development of cash-based market economies and capitalism. Weber has argued that modern or rational capitalism was 'oriented to market opportunities' developed 'on the basis of saleable services' (1927: 356). The basis of market relations are *competent* individuals who are capable of entering into contracts and of discharging their contractual obligations to other individuals and groups when required. The development of modern industrial society is thus closely associated with the development of an individualist ideology. Individualism emphasizes the centrality of the individual within society as an independent decision-making unit and sees the main basis of society as agreements between such individuals expressed in contractual form. As Maine pointed out children and mentally incompetent adults were explicitly excluded from such relations and: 'remain subject to extrinsic control on the single ground that they do not possess the faculty of forming a judgment on their own interests' (Maine 1866: 169–70).

The economic changes created by industrialization and the social changes implicit in the development of individualism, were accompanied by political changes, especially the emergence of nation states and liberal democracy in Europe and North America. In the early modern period, nation states were highly competitive, both economically and politically. In both types of competition the state was increasingly dependent upon, and therefore interested in, not just the élite but the whole of the (productive) population.

The key policy statements

As policy makers attempted to grapple with the social problems generated by the process of industrialization and urbanization, so the pace and scope of policy development increased, especially for children. Thus in the nineteenth century there was a range of legislation concerning different aspects of childhood, beginning with child specific health and safety legislation, then juvenile justice legislation, and finally child protection legislation. There was a similar growth in legislation concerning people with learning disabilities, though this was intertwined with both 'lunacy' and the Poor Law statutes.

Both legislative reform programmes reached a climax at the beginning of the twentieth century in the 1908 Children Act and the 1913 Mental Deficiency Act, which formed part of an overall programme of welfare reforms, frequently referred to as the 'Liberal Reforms' (Hay 1983). In the early modern period, therefore, we focused upon these policy developments, and the associated policy reviews, because they marked an important transition point, looking backwards and consolidating previous developments, but also looking forward, and provided the basic framework for policy during the first half of the twentieth century.

Policy and vulnerable people

Although the Children Act (1908) contained little which could be described as new it substantially set the legislative framework in respect of children for the next quarter of a century. Like feudal measures, the Act is primarily concerned with threats to society, especially from child crime. The main thrust of the 1908 Children Act was, therefore, to consolidate the law in respect of juvenile offenders. As Fox-Harding (1991) pointed out even the Act's protective measures, aimed at enhancing the welfare of children, were justified in terms of social benefits of promoting national security and economic efficiency – the high profile issues of the time. The Act depicted juvenile crime as a distinctive social threat, to be dealt with differently from adult crime, by establishing separate juvenile courts and restricting the punishments to which children and young persons could be sentenced. A child could be seen as an innocent victim, for example if found begging, wandering, destitute or in the care of an 'unfit' adult. However, such children were seen as presenting a similar threat to the offending child and were subject to the same forms of care and control. Thus all 'uncontrolled' children whether 'innocent' or criminal were controlled through the reformatory and industrial school.

These institutions were the last resort; the state's main concern was to ensure that the family was exerting proper control over its children. There developed a range of measures designed to police the family. Potentially neglectful or cruel parents were to be deterred from harming their children by coercive threats, while those who were not deterred were 'guilty of an offence', punishable by fines, imprisonment and, potentially, permanent separation from the child. Thus a primary mechanism for risk management adopted in the 1908 Children Act was one of blame and punishment; the criminalization of 'failing' parents.

Within the development of policy concerning adults with learning disabilities, there was a similar emphasis on the threat to society. Whereas in the case of children, there was a strong awareness that some children might be innocent victims, i.e. the threat might arise because of the failure of responsible adults especially their parents, in the case of people with learning disabilities, they were seen as the main source of the threat. The 1913 Mental Deficiency Act emphasized the risk to society. Although formally aimed at making *'Further and Better Provision for the Care* of Feeble-minded and other Mentally Defective Persons' (our italics) the Act's main emphasis was on 'control' rather than 'care' (Mental Deficiency Act 1913). For example, one objective of the Act was for local agencies to screen the communities for which they were responsible, identify all adults and children with learning disabilities, *regardless* of their need for care. As such, the Act established a formal identity of 'otherness', of alternative and lesser citizenship for the person with learning disabilities who, once having been categorized or certified as 'mentally defective' and a 'subject to be dealt with', could become the subject of supervision or potentially restrictive intervention, regardless of need. The establishment of a 'Board of *Control*' (our italics) emphasized that the main policy concern was protecting society rather than vulnerable people.

Administration and accountability

Legislators in the early twentieth century could build on the developments of the previous century, in particular they could make use of existing administrative structures. But there was a difference in emphasis between the 1908 Children Act and the 1913 Mental Deficiency Act. The 1913 Mental Deficiency Act involved a restructuring of administration, symbolized by the creation of new bodies such as the 'Board of Control'. It also fostered the development of institutional facilities as the main mechanism of care and control and therefore involved specification of responsibilities and accountabilities of agencies and their employees. Although the 1908 Children Act involved the development of existing roles, for example, administrators who could remove children to a 'place of safety', and also included institutional provision in the form of special types of school, its emphasis was on the effective management of children in the family. Thus there was less specification of roles and responsibilities and more overt legal control of children and families.

In learning disability, the institution provided the main focus of accountability. The actions or inactions of the employees of the Institution were punishable under the Act as criminal offences with specified penalties, generally fines and/or imprisonment. For example, hiding a person in an institution or allowing or encouraging a 'patient' to escape was an offence punishable by a fine of up to £50 or imprisonment of up to three months. The 1913 Act also explicitly listed those who carried responsibility for the care of a person with a learning disability and therefore were accountable. This included patients' families as well as the emerging caring professions (para. 55).

Under the 1908 Children Act, the institution was also an important focus of accountability. For example, reformatory and industrial schools were required to register and to have annual inspections (paras 45 and 46), and certificates could be withdrawn. However, accountability was more general; all citizens, not just employees of the schools, could be prosecuted if they were cruel to the children in their charge. The general legislation applied to 'any person over the age of sixteen years, who has the custody, charge, or care of any child or younger person' (para. 12).

Thus under both Acts, institutions were given a central role in the identification and management of risk. Employees of these institutions had a specific responsibility for protecting society by ensuring that dangerous individuals were placed and retained in appropriate facilities. Although they also had a responsibility for protecting vulnerable individuals by ensuring they were not harmed, this was not as clearly specified as their responsibility for protecting society.

Comment

The Industrial Revolution was associated not only with major economic changes but parallel social and political changes; the context in which early modern policy developments occurred was therefore characterized by increasing complexity. These contextual changes were reflected in increasingly complex official perceptions of vulnerable people, the ways in which their dependency was seen as a social problem and the ways in which this problem should be managed.

Underlying the Liberal reforms is an 'equality of vulnerability'. Whereas the type and level of threat and risk posed by vulnerable people in the feudal system varied according to their position in the social system, as did the state response to the threat, in the Liberal reforms a similar pattern of risk was associated with each category of vulnerable person and the nature of the problem became more complex. In the feudal system, the prime concern of the state was with the maintenance of social order and stability. In the early modern period, this concern was still prominent but there was also a greater concern with protecting the vulnerable individual, particularly children, and thus there were concerns not only with dealing with the effects of vulnerability but also understanding the causes so that preventive action could be taken. Thus the welfare of individual children or adults and their vulnerability to abuse became a theme, albeit one which at times remained subordinate to concerns about societal protection.

The growth of state concern with the social problems posed by vulnerable individuals in society was accompanied by the emergence and development of modern caring professions and of institutions as the major mechanism for managing risks both to and from vulnerable people. Policy makers delegated a prime role in risk management to institutions and their employees who accumulated specific roles and powers in relationship to vulnerable people. There was also a clearer specification of professional accountability to the law, i.e. a specification of actions which could constitute criminal offences and the punishments for these offences. The duty to protect society, e.g. by keeping the vulnerable person in the proper place, was clearly specified and the punishments clearly outlined. In contrast, responsibility for protecting the vulnerable person from abuse was more diffuse and generalized.

POLICY IN LATE MODERN SOCIETY

Context

In the late twentieth century, there have again been major economic changes. Technological innovations have transformed communications, production and markets. These changes have had social impacts. Industries no longer need huge amounts of unskilled labour concentrated in large centres of population but instead there is a demand for highly skilled labour. Contemporary society is marked by breakdown of the rural/urban divide.

The development of late modern society is associated with the development of welfare states, especially in Northern Europe. Viewed from the perspective of risk, the welfare state is as a mechanism by which individual risk, e.g. of ill health or unemployment, is collectively shared either through insurance-based systems or state funded systems (Giddens 1994). The reasons for the development of such systems are a subject for dispute. As Giddens (1990: 114) pointed out one of the explanations may be the changing nature of risk. Modern technologies may be effective at managing risk at individual level, e.g. the development of antibiotics may reduce both the incidence and impact of infectious diseases, but may increase the risks at global level, e.g. confidence in antibiotics may create changes in both human behaviour and the nature of micro-organisms that result in global epidemics. These global risks require collective action.

The changing nature of economic production also plays a role. Globalization is associated with the development of autonomous multi-national or transnational corporations (Giddens 1993: 543–51); nation states attract their capital investment by providing a disciplined, healthy and skilled work force and by absorbing the costs of sustaining this work force. They can also enhance their attractiveness by grouping together in free trade zones, such as the European Union. Both these trends enhance the state's concern with the welfare and well-being of individual contractual employees.

As nation states such as the United Kingdom have lost control over economic activity (to transnational economic corporations) and political activity (to multi-national political groupings), so their role as collective risk managers, through the provision of welfare, has become increasingly important, and welfare expenditure now dominates government spending. The criteria by which the performance of nation states are judged are also increasingly globalized and this can be seen in the adoption of international concepts such as civil rights and associated ideologies of welfare such as 'normalization'. The importance of welfare for the international identity of the nation state has resulted in a move away from narrow concerns with employees and towards wider concerns with all citizens. Thus in late modern society, policies in respect of risk and vulnerable people are formulated within an even more complex context. This complexity is reflected in contemporary official perceptions of vulnerable people, the ways in which risks are associated with vulnerability and the mechanisms whereby those risks should be managed.

Key policy statements

Two key documents make up the current policy framework in England with regard to vulnerable children and risk: the Children Act 1989, with its accompanying guidance and regulations, and *Working Together* (Home Office *et al.* 1991), which provides guidance for cooperation and collaboration between professionals to facilitate the protection of children from abuse. In contrast, the learning disability policy framework remains dispersed and is contained within a variety of general pronouncements which outline the broad responsibilities of health and social service providers to a range of service user groups. Although it was published a quarter of a century ago, the White Paper *Better Services for the Mentally Handicapped* (Department of Health and Social Security and Welsh Office 1971) remains a key policy statement for adults with learning disability, while the White Paper *Caring for People* (Department of Health 1989a) establishes current patterns of service delivery. Both confirm the shift in emphasis from managing risk through institutions to managing risk in the community. Though the issue of risk takes on greater significance as vulnerable adults move from institutional care to the less protective environment of the community, neither of these White Papers explicitly addresses risk, or its management, unlike the childcare framework where assessing and managing the risk of abuse is a major theme.

Policy and vulnerable people

As we have discussed above, although historically policy makers have recognized the vulnerability of adults with learning disabilities and children, they have traditionally been conceptualized, and responded to, primarily in terms of the risks which their vulnerability potentially poses to society. In this section, we consider the extent to which these dual themes of dangerousness and vulnerability are evident in contemporary policy before considering a theme which is new to the late modern period, the social incorporation of vulnerable people, in particular the official conceptualization of vulnerable people as 'takers of risk'.

Vulnerable people as threat to society

Policy in the late modern period is characterized by a decline in emphasis on the social threat posed by vulnerable people. In relation to people with learning disabilities, Alaszewski (1988) has delineated this move from an official identity as 'villains' to one as 'victims'. For this group, concerns at national level relate mainly to the implications of 'challenging behaviour' in the context of the move towards community care. These concerns have been demonstrated at national level by the establishment of the Mansell Committee, which reported to the Department of Health in 1992 (Mansell 1993). Although children who are 'beyond parental control', are explicitly identified in the 1989 Children Act (s31(2)), the main emphasis of the legislation is upon the welfare of children. Nevertheless, concerns about vulnerable people as posing a potential social threat still exist, and surface occasionally (but significantly) in debates around high profile incidents such as the killing of James Bulger by two children.

The protection of vulnerable people from abuse

There is a major difference in emphasis between policy relating to people with a learning disability and children in respect of protection from abuse. Whereas this is a relatively minor (but important) theme within policy for people with a learning disability, it is the dominant theme in child care policy.

In policy for people with a learning disability, the issue of abuse comes up particularly in relationship to sexuality. For example, the government response to the House of Commons Social Services Select Committee report on community care recognized 'the vulnerability of some mentally handicapped people to sexual abuse by other people' (cited in Department of Health and Social Security 1985 para. 30). Responsibility for managing this risk was delegated to local agencies and their staff, with the suggestion that such vulnerable service users should be supported by 'sensitive professional work by staff' (Department of Health and Social Security 1985, para. 30).

In contrast, concerns about the abuse of children have been a major factor in the development of policy for children. It is a pervasive theme in the Children Act 1989 and the dominant theme in *Working Together*. This emphasis on protecting children is also evident in other accompanying national policy advice. For example, *Protecting Children* contained the following statement:

> *[t]he first duty of a social worker* in a child protection agency, working within the framework of statutory powers, *is to ensure the child's protection* and then to promote his or her physical, emotional and intellectual health and development.
>
> (Department of Health 1988, para. 4.3, our italics)

Thus the guidance given in national documents to professionals working with vulnerable children and their families focuses professional attention upon protection.

The social integration of vulnerable people

It is possible to identify a new concern in policy, i.e. the harm which social exclusion creates, particularly if individuals are placed in socially segregated and isolated settings such as institutions. Institutions, whose formal objective was to protect vulnerable people (and society), are now seen as increasing vulnerability and dependency.

For people with learning disabilities the emphasis in policy on social integration is both explicit and well developed. This emphasis on social integration is closely associated with the acceptance and official endorsement of the 'normalization' principle (Wolfensberger 1980), in which user participation and empowerment are major objectives of service provision.

A requirement upon professionals to involve vulnerable adults in the assessment process was specifically prioritized by policy makers in *Caring for People* (Department of Health 1989a), which asserted the general principle that service users should be enabled to achieve 'control over their own lives' (para. 2.2), in other words they should be enabled to exercise choice. However, as Wright, Haycox and Leedham noted, '[t]here is a conflict between the need for risk taking and the need for protection, and a need for an optimal balance between over protection and under protection' (1994: 56).

In childcare policy, the emphasis upon social integration is more implicit, both because of the emphasis on abuse and because the child is part of a family. The integration is therefore both of the child within the family and the family within society. However, a similar tension for professionals, between under and over protection, can also be discerned within the child protection policy framework.

The Children Act 1989 is founded upon the principle of preserving family autonomy and a particular focus of concern is the balance between the right of families not to be subjected to unnecessary state interference and the potentially conflicting right of children to be protected from harm (Department of Health 1989b, para. 6.2). The task of achieving this balance is delegated to professionals, particularly social workers, who must weigh the relative consequences of intervention/non-intervention, bearing in mind that unnecessary intervention may be harmful to the whole family, but failure to intervene may result in harm to the child. If the balance has been achieved, risk has been managed effectively, if not the potential costs to the child, family and professional are high. However, consistently achieving this balance requires the accurate identification of children 'at risk' and reliable assessment of the degree of risk to which they are exposed. Evidence suggests that this represents a difficult, if not impossible search for perfection (Parton 1985, Dingwall 1989; Parton 1989).

Professional roles and accountability

Contemporary policy therefore constructs a triple official identity in respect of both adults with learning disabilities and children – threat to society, vulnerablity to abuse and vulnerability to social exclusion. This has resulted in a series of potentially contradictory policy objectives which may be classified as protecting society, protecting the individual and empowering the individual and the family. Responsibility for achieving these policy objectives has been delegated by policy-makers to front-line workers, especially professionals.

The difficult judgements which staff have to make when reconciling competing policy objectives were clearly recognized by the Jay Committee (Report of the Committee of Enquiry into Mental Handicap Nursing and Care 1979), in respect of people with learning disabilities:

> Staff are likely to receive harsh criticism when accident or injury occurs, yet if we entirely cushion people against these dangers we immediately restrict their lives and their chances of development. This restriction can be cloaked in respectability and defended on the grounds of protecting mentally handicapped people and keeping them safe, but it can also endanger human dignity. Each of us lives in a world which is not always safe, secure and predictable; mentally handicapped people need to assume a fair and prudent share of risk.
>
> (1979: para. 121)

This paragraph encapsulated the fundamental tension for professionals when seeking to protect an individual's right to autonomy, while also protecting him or her from harm. To this one could add the responsibility of professionals to protect society.

However, national policy statements, particularly those in respect of adults with learning disabilities, offer little guidance on how a balance between competing policy objectives might be achieved. This is left to operational policy, and to managers and staff at local level. In respect of children, *Working Together* offers guidance, but the task of establishing local procedures for dealing with suspected and confirmed cases of maltreatment to children is delegated to Area Child Protection Committees (ACPCs).

These increasingly complex official understandings of risk in respect of vulnerable people have arisen within the context of more extensive and highly pressured mechanisms of professional accountability. To examine the impact of the tensions in national policy it is therefore important to consider the ways in which professionals are held to account. There are four main mechanisms; the law, professional bodies, public inquiries and the media.

The law
In both the pre-modern and early modern periods the law formed the major mechanism of accountability. With the dismantling of the institutions and the associated legal framework, the significance of the law has declined, but it remains important as a default mechanism. For example, when adults with learning disabilities are cared for in residential accommodation, much care is provided by unqualified staff, the main mechanism of accountability is through legislation governing such facilities and general health and safety legislation (for example the Registered Homes Act 1984, the Nursing Homes and Mental Nursing Homes Regulations 1984 para. 12 (1) (s), Council of Europe 89/391/EEC, 12.6.89, Articles 5 and 9 and the Health and Safety at Work Act 1974, para. 7a).

Professional bodies
Given the growth of welfare professions, their use by the state for risk management and their dominance in providing public support for vulnerable people, a major instrument of accountability is self-regulation of professions. Those professions that have registration bodies have codes of professional ethics or conduct, which provide a clear framework for accountability. This can be seen in nursing, for example.

Through the Nurses, Midwives and Health Visitors Act (1979) all registered nurses are subject to the United Kingdom Central Council (UKCC) for Nursing, Midwifery and Health Visiting. Its *Code of Professional Conduct* (UKCC 1992) establishes the standards and framework for professional practice. The Code is not a legal document; it has the status of guidance, but if its requirements are not met a registered nurse may be removed or suspended from the Register. The Code therefore represents a powerful influence upon practice and has implications for the ways in which nurses manage risk. For example the introductory paragraph of the Code of Conduct states that:

> Each registered nurse, midwife and health visitor shall act, at all times, in such a manner as to:
> • *safeguard* and promote the interests of individual patients and clients.
> (UKCC 1992, our italics)

This appears to promote a paternalistic rather than empowering approach to risk taking by service users, implying a protective, best-interests oriented strategy of care. However the Code also requires nurses to:

> work in an open and co-operative manner with patients, clients and their families, *foster their independence and recognise and respect their involvement in the planning and delivery of care.*
> (UKCC 1992 para. 5, our italics)

Thus the Code of Conduct also endorses the participation and empowerment of service users. Young (1994) highlighted the tension experienced by nurses managing risk-taking behaviour, when a vulnerable person wishes to undertake an activity which may result in harm. The registered nurse is faced with a choice between the professional duty of care on the one hand and civil liberties issues on the other, both of which are endorsed within the 'Code of Conduct'.

Inquiries

The public inquiry system is a formal and highly visible mechanism for scrutinizing professional decision making. Public inquiries have been used in the field of learning disability (Report of the Committee of Inquiry into Allegations of Ill-Treatment of Patients and other irregularities at the Ely Hospital Cardiff 1969; Report of the Committee of Inquiry into Normansfield Hospital 1978), but their findings with regard to professional decision making and vulnerable children have been far more numerous and achieved greater notoriety.

Reder and colleagues (1993) have reviewed inquiry reports into child death as a result of carer abuse between 1973 and 1989. They concluded that although the intention of the panels was not to seek individual scapegoats, nevertheless 'there can be little doubt that discovering who was to blame dominated many of the panels' thinking' (1993: 135), and this blame has tended to fall upon fieldworkers (particularly social workers, but also health professionals) and their managers.

The media

The media has played an important role in informing the public about social work and social workers, particularly in relation to child protection. Considerably less media interest is shown towards adults with learning disabilities, unless mental illness is also an issue. In both cases, media attention has tended to be almost exclusively negative, focusing upon situations where professionals 'got it wrong' (Aldridge 1994, Jackson, *et al.* 1995). This is not to suggest that it is inappropriate for professionals and their employing agencies to be the subject of media scrutiny, but rather that this apparently unfair and unbalanced representation of some professional practice may itself be detrimental to vulnerable service users and their families.

A recurrent theme within the child protection literature is that fear of a critical media is a powerful contributory factor to defensive practice for both front-line staff and social work managers (Jackson *et al.* 1995, Reder *et al.* 1993). Dale *et al.* (cited in Parton and Parton 1989) have identified the phenomenon of 'professional dangerousness', whereby persistent and public negative criticism contributes to anxious and uncertain professional practice thereby, paradoxically, increasing the levels of risk to which children are exposed.

Comment

Major technical, economic, social and political changes have occurred in the twentieth century. These have been associated with more complex official understandings of the risks posed by, and to, vulnerable people and more sophisticated mechanisms for risk management. Official concerns about the overall threat to society posed by vulnerable people have declined and this has led to a reduction in the importance of identifying and isolating such individuals, except specific individuals who have additional criminal or challenging behaviours.

Within policy, it is possible to identify three objectives, which are potentially contradictory; the concern to protect society against the dangers presented by (some) vulnerable/dangerous individuals; the concern to protect vulnerable individuals from abuse; and the concern to incorporate vulnerable individuals within ordinary social relations and give them the same opportunities as other individuals. There are different emphases in child care and services for adults with a learning disability. Child care is dominated by concerns over the vulnerability of the child, especially to abuse. For adults with learning disabilities the major concern is social exclusion which needs to be countered by providing individuals with opportunities to participate in and take the risks of ordinary life.

The management of these potentially contradictory objectives is delegated to welfare professionals but the policy statements in which they are constructed contain little specific guidance on how the tension between competing policy objectives can, or should be managed. Professionals are expected to use their judgement to manage the contradictions, but at the same time are increasingly held to account for their actions and inactions. Although there is less emphasis on specific legal mechanisms, there has been a development of professional bodies and their scrutiny of professional practice. The inquiry system provides a means for central or local government to investigate situations where harm has occurred. Underlying all these mechanisms is the growth of media interest in, and concern about, professional practice. We will return to issues of professional accountability in Chapter 5.

CONCLUSION

It is clear that vulnerable people have been conceptualized as a 'social problem' from an early period but official perceptions about the nature of the problem, and therefore the appropriate state response, have changed.

In the feudal period the 'problem' was relatively straightforward. Although there was official recognition of the potential risks of exploitation to which vulnerable people (within the élite at least) were exposed, the major concern was with the threat which vulnerability posed to social order, either because it potentially threatened the long-term security of property and property rights or because of its association with destitution and crime. These two separate threats were associated with separate solutions; the first was dealt with by providing mechanisms to protect property and inheritance, and the second by taking measures to ensure that 'criminals', and beggars whether vulnerable or otherwise, were brought to justice.

The early modern period was marked by social, economic and political dislocation and the growth of government power. The growth of size and scale of the social problems associated with vulnerability was linked with growing governmental capacity to deal with the problems. Although initial responses to vulnerability built on and developed pre-modern responses, increasingly there was a concern to identify the causes of vulnerability and take action to protect the vulnerable.

The Liberal reforms represented a reconceptualization of the social problems created by vulnerability. The dominant theme within this conceptualization remained the threat to social order and stability, however, with changing patterns of social relations, the perceived nature of the threat had changed. The growth of individualism meant that vulnerable people tended to be outside of, and a threat to, contractual relations within modern society. In the early modern period, the two main objectives of policy – protecting society and protecting the individual – were to be attained through the institutions and the emerging caring professions that managed them. Institutions were designed to manage risks to society by segregating vulnerable (and potentially dangerous) individuals and to reduce the risk to vulnerable individuals by placing them in safe and secure environments. Thus the emerging caring professions took lead responsibility for managing risks to and from vulnerable people, primarily using the defined space of institutions (see Alaszewski *et al.* 1997). Since protecting society tended to be the dominant objective, the accountability of the emerging care professions was more clearly defined in relationship to the institution, i.e. preventing vulnerable people leaving rather than in protecting vulnerable people from abuse.

In the late modern period, there has been a further change in the nature of economic and social relations. Both capital and the associated skilled labour are becoming more and more mobile and nation-states must increasingly compete to obtain and retain both. In advanced industrial democracies, one of the major mechanisms for achieving this is through the social incorporation of all citizens. Thus in the late modern period, concerns about the threat to society posed by vulnerable people are increasingly replaced by concerns about individual exploitation or violence and the social exclusion of vulnerable people. Thus, there is a concern to empower individuals by offering them the opportunity of an 'ordinary' life, for example by including people with learning disabilities in the labour market.

These changing emphases within policy mean that the main mechanism developed during the early modern period for caring for and controlling individuals, i.e. the institution, is no longer acceptable, and increasingly caring professionals are directly and individually responsible for reconciling conflicting policy objectives. Central to their successful accomplishment of this task is their ability to assess and reconcile various forms of risk: risk to society; risk to the vulnerable individual; and the empowerment of vulnerable individuals to take risks.

PART 2

AGENCIES AND RISK

WELFARE AGENCIES AND RISK: FORMAL STRUCTURES AND STRATEGIES

Andy Alaszewski and Jill Manthorpe

A rapid growth of interest in risk analysis, assessment and management has characterized the development of care and support for vulnerable people living in the community. However, attention has mainly focused on the roles and activities of individual professionals who provide or supervise care and support. In this chapter we extend the debate by examining the role of welfare agencies in the processes of assessing and managing risk.

ORGANIZATIONS AND RISK

Agencies provide the link between national policy and front-line worker practice.There is a growing body of literature analysing the role of professionals in managing various types of risks in the community. This perspective encompasses research, policy and practice. When disasters occur in health and welfare, individuals are seriously harmed or even die, then subsequent investigations often identify that agency and interagency structures and relationships are important contributory factors (Department of Health and Social Security 1982). However, both the analysis of the ways in which agencies actually work, and their recommendations for improved working are limited. For example, the recommendations of the Butler-Sloss Inquiry (1988) into child protection issues in Cleveland were a mixture of exhortation to better cooperation and calls for the formalization, or bureaucratization, of interagency relations (Alaszewski and Harrison 1988: 642).

It is therefore surprising that the role of agencies in identifying and managing risk has been relatively neglected. For example, Billis (1984) examined the structure of welfare bureaucracies such as social services departments, and concluded that their structure is a crucial element in shaping professional practice. Although he provided a case study of decision making (pp. 189–98) (though not risk), his discussion is both abstract and prescriptive so it is not clear how agencies actually structure decision making and risk management. Coulshed (1990), in her study of management in social work, also examined decision making. Although she did not explicitly discuss risk, she did note that managers often had to 'choose between different courses of action in a climate of uncertainty' (p. 97). She also discussed decision tree analysis, one decision-support system which can be used to manage risk. Coulshed did not examine the ways in which the agency context influences the decision-making process and risk management. Dowie and Elstein (1988), in their reader on decision making, analyse risk and decision making and include a section on the context of decision making which addresses the professional context but does not address the agency context.

In the remainder of this chapter we shall develop a conceptual framework for analysing the strategic choices which agencies can make. In the final section, this framework is analysed using data from a survey of welfare agencies.

DEVELOPING A CONCEPTUAL FRAMEWORK

Until the 1980s, there was very little analysis of the ways in which welfare agencies managed risk. In so far as risk was considered, it tended to be in specialist areas such as financial management or health and safety. These are important areas in welfare agencies, but they only indirectly relate to the risk management of core activities: providing service user care and support.

Since the analysis of risk management by health and welfare agencies is a recent development, it is possible to provide a framework by re-examining, from a risk perspective, some of the classic works on organizations in general and welfare agencies in particular. We first consider the risk implications of Weber's ideal type organizations and Goffman's study of asylums. Then we consider more recent work which focuses on the management of risk, especially the work of Hood and colleagues on 'doctrinal contests' in risk management.

WEBERIAN IDEAL TYPES

The seminal work of Max Weber (1947) remains an important influence on the analysis of organizations. Weber argued that organizations are based on co-operation between individuals. In modern societies, with their individualistic ideologies, he identified two main reasons why individuals cooperate, and therefore two patterns of cooperation. One is based on reason or rationality, and the other on the personal charisma of a leader. Rational cooperation is based on explicit and agreed goals. These goals are publicly stated in a formal or legal document that specifies the purposes of cooperation which is intended to achieve these ends. This type of authority underpins modern bureaucratic organizations. In contrast, charisma is the personal qualities of a leader and individuals cooperate because they accept this charismatic authority. The

Box 3.1: Weber's ideal types and their risk implications

	Bureaucratic	*Charismatic*
General characteristics	• Impersonal • Structured • Rule-oriented • Closed	• Personal • Fluid • Spontaneous • Open
Risk characteristics	• Risk averse • Expert-oriented • Tendency towards punishment • Closed to the environment	• Risk prone • Non-expert • Reward for success • Open to the environment

divine inspiration of a religious leader is not justified by reason but by the faith of his or her followers.

Weber defined bureaucracy as a hierarchical structure of office-holders who make decisions based on impersonal rules. Because of this, bureaucracies tend to be order-oriented, primarily concerned with maintaining stability and predictability; they tend to emphasize the possible harm that can come from risk-taking rather than the potential benefits. Cooperation based on charisma is not organized around formal rigid structures but forms a network of personal relations focused on the central charismatic individual. This type of organization is associated with both considerable fluidity and uncertainty and can be seen as providing the context for spontaneity and creativity, it thrives on and indeed fosters risk. The main differences are summarized in Box 3.1.

Weber's classic study of authority remains a continuing influence in the study of organizations and underlies many typologies. For example, Burns and Stalker's (1961) classification of organizations into mechanistic and organic can be seen as a development of Weber's analysis. Burns and Stalker identify bureaucracy-like mechanistic organizations with rigid hierarchical structures. These work well in relatively stable environments with low levels of change and limited competition. They provide maximum control, but minimum flexibility, as they do not provide incentives for taking the risks which are a prerequisite for innovation.

In more turbulent environments, with rapid technological innovation or high levels of competition between organizations, a more flexible structure is required. 'Organic' organizations have horizontal links and use flexible, task-oriented teams. These teams take responsibility for specific areas of activity and develop their own creative solutions to specific problems. The emphasis is on rapid and creative responses to specific threats and opportunities. This flexible type of organization, with its liberation of individual creativity, has

Box 3.2: King, Raynes and Tizard's typology of childcare agencies		
	Staff centred	*Child centred*
General characteristics	• Hierarchical and centralized control • Formality and distance between staff and residents • Batch control of residents • Isolated from the community	• Autonomy for unit head • Informality and closeness of staff and children • Individualized treatment of children • Integrated into the community
Risk implications	• Emphasis on safety • Strong professional or expert culture • Punishment orientation • Closed, protected environment	• Client choice • More emphasis on the role of lay people • Emphasis on learning • Open to outside influences

become a central feature of much current organizational design and managerial thinking (see for example, Morgan 1993).

Goffman and the study of health and welfare organizations

Most organizational theory literature is based on studies of private sector or public administrative organizations. There is a parallel literature on welfare or caring organizations, but this tends to be based on descriptive studies of organizations, both case studies (see, for example, Alaszewski 1986; Rapaport 1960; MacAndrew and Edgerton 1964) and surveys (see, for example, Tizard *et al.* 1975 and Miller and Gwynne 1972), rather than theoretical constructions. Goffman's classic study (1961) of the Asylum builds on this empirical literature providing it with a theoretical structure. There are similarities between Goffman's ideal type of the asylum and Weber's administrative bureaucracy. Goffman's asylum has a rigid hierarchical structure based on the inflexible application of rules and procedures which are designed to process inmates with minimal cost. It manages external risk by insulating itself from its environment and manages internal risks through the application of a rigid institutional regimen which makes overt inmate resistance virtually impossible.

Although Goffman provided just one ideal type, King and colleagues (1971) used it to develop a typology. They classified residential units providing care for children with a learning disability into staff-centred and child-centred. Staff-centred units were asylum-like with rigid, rule-oriented, hierarchical structures which distanced staff from the children they cared for, thus providing a justification for the impersonal and the 'batch' management of children. In contrast, child-centred facilities were decentralized allowing autonomy and flexibility to the head of the unit. Within such units the emphasis was on individualized childcare and support. Thus these units encouraged higher levels of individual freedom and choice, and by implication associated risks (see Box 3.2).

Hood's typology of risk management

Both the Weberian and the Goffman approaches use ideal types which attempt to capture the overall nature of specific organizations. Typologies based on their work tend to stress the difference between two opposed ideal types such as mechanistic versus organic structures or staff-centred versus client-centred agencies. This approach to organizations remains influential and can be seen in Hood and colleagues' (1992) survey of the literature on organizational management of risk.

Hood and colleagues argued (1992: 158–67) that there were seven distinctive 'doctrinal contests' or dimensions of organizations' response to risk. These seven contests were:

- *narrow versus broad participation*: the extent to which decision-making is restricted to experts or open to broader participation;
- *assigning blame versus absolving*: the extent to which the organization blames staff to encourage 'safety' or has a no-fault approach to encourage learning;
- *anticipation versus rapid response*: the extent to which the organization emphasizes anticipation of or response to risk;
- *quantification versus qualitativism*: the extent to which the organization emphasizes the use of quantitative data as the basis for decisions or accepts that key aspects are unquantifiable;
- *design versus laissez-faire*: the extent to which the organization uses explicit organizational design as the basis of its structure and decision making;
- *safety as an absolute goal versus safety as part of a trade off*: the extent to which safety is seen as an absolute goal or can be traded off against other goals in decision making;
- *outcome versus process specification*: the extent to which the regulatory process focuses on the outcome or the process of organizational decision making.

Although all these doctrinal contests are potentially important, some are more important to the operation of welfare agencies than others. For example, the issue of 'design' is clearly relevant to the development of systems such as aircrafts, in which the interaction between the pilot and the technology is crucial, and human error can be counteracted by a computer system. However, as welfare agencies are human systems which make limited use of technology in decision making, design is not a crucial issue. Similarly, the contest between outcome and process specification may be of theoretical importance in welfare agencies but given the absence of outcome measures, regulatory systems focus on process and input. We shall therefore discuss three contests which are of particular importance to the ways in which *welfare agencies* respond to risk and where real choice exists: participation in decision-making, the allocation of blame and the anticipation of risk.

Participation in decision making
Hood and colleagues (1992) argued that organizations either treated risk as a highly technical matter, and therefore rely exclusively on expert advice, or they saw it as including wider issues of values and therefore sought to widen participation in decision making.

If risk is primarily defined as a highly technical matter, then the organization needs to draw on the special knowledge and skills of professionals or experts to assess probabilities and to effectively assess and manage risk. For example, Yalow (1985) argued for the restriction of decision making to scientifically well-informed participants. He considered that this would ensure that rational and rigorous decision making was not swamped by ill-informed contributors. Furthermore, individual experts advocating a risky project would not be able to diffuse responsibility. The responsibility for decisions clearly rests with experts, who may be more easily held to account. In mental health, for example, there have been calls to abolish the power of lay managers under the Mental Health Act 1983 to uphold appeals against detention by 'sectioned' patients in the face of their doctors' wish to maintain the detention.

However, organizations which rely on experts or professionals must trust these experts and their judgement. It is clear that professionals and other experts are no longer automatically trusted following preventable disasters such as thalidomide. Perhaps this loss of trust can be most clearly seen in environmental issues. The risks associated with DDT and other pesticides, in particular their cumulation in the food chain and the resulting demise of predatory birds, which are at the end of the food chain, such as the American Bald Eagle, were initially noted by amateur ornithologists. These risks were publicized by Rachel Carson (1962), a popular writer with a scientific back-ground. Moreover, Hood and colleagues (1992) pointed out that there is often no consensus among experts. There is a plurality of competencies in which the claims of any one particular expert may be called into question by another (Hood *et al.* 1992: 164). For example, many of the recent panics about the safety of food such as 'mad cow disease' (bovine spongiform encephalopathy) are associated with public disagreements between experts (Miller and Reilly 1994). It can also be argued that broader participation increases the account-ability of technical decision makers to the community (Beder 1991) and is morally superior (Hood *et al.* 1992: 164).

Allocating blame: internal management and reward systems
Hood and colleagues (1992) argued that organizations can use internal incen-tive systems to manage risk in different ways. Organizations can either have systems which focus on the allocation of responsibility and blame, or systems which emphasize the importance of learning from rather than punishing mistakes.

Punitive systems are based on negative sanctions. Within organizations using such systems, primary concerns are accountability, and allocating responsibility or blame when incidents occur. This is intended to provide employees with clear incentives for, and biases towards, safety (Hood *et al.* 1992: 159). However, such an approach also provides employees with an incentive to cover-up. Thus an investigation into a major aircraft accident in the USA found 'a number of previous near accidents with similar causal factors' (Tait 1996: 1) but these had not been reported. As a result the USA developed a confidential system for reporting which formed the basis of one in the UK, the Confidential Human Factors Incident Reporting Programme (CHIRP). The aim of these systems is to learn from minor incidents and thus prevent accidents. To get the necessary information, the agency must provide some protection, offer confidentiality, for individuals who report incidents so that these individuals are absolved from blame. In the case of CHIRP, the Deputy Director identified the factors in the following way:

> For any confidential reporting system to be successful, it is imperative that it is able to demonstrate clearly to the relevant user groups that it is functionally and managerially totally independent of the systems to which the reports will be submitted.
>
> (Burgess 1996)

In welfare agencies, the key process is the investigation of incidents and accidents. The approach taken by agencies is often related to the status of the professional staff involved, and therefore the implicit extent to which their judgement is trusted, and they are permitted to regulate themselves and investigate their own short-comings. Thus social workers have not had a self-regulating system, although this is due to change with the announcement of the formation of a General Social Care Council (Guy 1994; Department of Health 1996). Their errors are subject to both external review by inquiries and the media. At the other extreme is the medical profession, which enjoys a high professional status and has traditionally been allowed high level of self-regulation. Accidents and incidents tend to be investigated by the profession itself using confidential inquiries, for example, homicides and suicides among psychiatric patients (Boyd 1996). However, studies of whistle-blowing in the NHS (Hunt 1995 and Public Concern at Work 1997) indicate that there is considerable room for developing further confidential, no-blame reporting systems.

Anticipation or response: managing the environment
The third main area in which organizations differ in their response to risk is in their relationship to their environments. Hood and colleagues (1992) argued that organizations could either attempt to predict or anticipate risks in order to prevent accidents, or they may view accidents as difficult, or even impossible, to predict and therefore develop mechanisms for responding rapidly when they have occurred to minimize the resulting harm.

Anticipation is very much the common sense strategy in which an organization seeks to identify all possible hazards, and to take action to prevent incidents occurring. The main emphasis is on assessing potential hazards. This approach dominates the approach advocated by the National Health Service Executive. For example, an NHS Hospital Trust risk policy document, which uses the NHS guidelines as a basis, equates risk with hazard. It states that one of the key objectives of the policy is to 'ensure an environment that poses the minimum of risk possible, for both staff and visitors' and risk is defined in negative terms 'as the possibility of incurring misfortune or loss' (St James and Seacroft University Hospitals 1995: 1–2). The danger inherent in this approach is that it can create a false sense of security. An organization may have such confidence in its ability to predict that it does not develop any measures to deal with accidents when they occur. If accidents happen, then their effects are likely to be magnified and become disasters. For example, the 'unsinkable' *Titanic* did not have sufficient lifeboats for all its passengers and crew. Many disasters are predictable *but only with hindsight* when all the available information has been brought together (Wildavsky 1985; Wildavsky 1988). Public inquiries into child abuse cases illustrate this well; they identify actions which could have been taken to prevent serious harm to a child, but they report that the appropriate action was not taken because the information which might have enabled effective prediction and action was at the time of the abuse dispersed between a number of organizations (DHSS 1982).

If an organization is not confident in its ability to predict then it may develop a 'rapid response' strategy based on early identification and swift response to harmful events. This tends to be a generalized response strategy. Since it will not be confident in its ability to anticipate and prevent specific types of harm, it will develop a general capacity to respond to different problems. This approach now dominates in child protection where there has been a shift from preventative work, attempting to identify all at-risk children, to rapid response to risk which is defined in terms of possible or actual harm (see, for example, Parton 1996). Nevertheless, social workers are criticized for responding to only one type of harm, parental abuse (Brandon *et al.* 1996: 19).

Comment

If these three areas are considered together (see Box 3.3), then they can be linked to both the Weberian ideal types and the typology developed by King, Raynes and Tizard. Traditional bureaucracy and staff-centred welfare organizations share common characteristics. In such organizations, there is likely to be a reliance on expert advice, an emphasis on punishing mistakes and an attempt to control the environment by anticipating hazards and risks. Charisma is essentially a personal quality and in its pure form cannot provide the basis of stable organizations; it therefore requires some stabilization. Organizations which emphasize the importance of individual judgement and contribution will tend to be more fluid and organic as envisaged by Burns and Stalker (1981), or client-centred welfare agencies identified by King and colleagues (1971). Such organizations are more likely to have a commitment to wider participation in decision making, especially involving service users, and encouraging organizational development through learning from minor mistakes; and are flexible, the anticipation of risk is balanced with rapid response to potentially harmful incidents.

We now examine whether the conceptual framework we have developed can be used as a framework for analysing the ways in which welfare agencies respond to risk.

Box 3.3: Key elements of three doctrinal contests		
Participation in decision making	*Narrow* • emphasis on expert judgement • relatively secret process • emphasis on the technical elements	*Broad* • emphasis on lay opinion • relatively open process • importance of value judgements
Internal incentive systems	*Blame* • emphasis on individual accountability • clear sanctions to provide a bias towards safety • mechanisms for allocating blame	*Absolution* • emphasis on organizational learning • protection for staff who report 'genuine' errors • incentives for sharing information
Managing the environment	*Anticipation* • organizational environment seen as controllable • emphasis on assessing hazards and taking preventative action	*Response* • organizational environment seen as unpredictable • emphasis on rapid reaction to a varied range of incidents

THE RECOGNITION AND MANAGEMENT OF RISK BY WELFARE AGENCIES

The study

The data reported here is derived from a survey of 42 agencies providing care for vulnerable children and adults with learning disabilities in the former Yorkshire Health region.

To select our agencies we first identified the population of agencies providing care and support and then selected a sample from this population. The population was identified by examining several data bases, such as the Social Services Year Book, to identify the addresses of agencies in the region. We identified over 900 addresses. About one third of these were either duplicates,

Table 3.1: Background information on survey of agencies

	Agencies	Response
Multipurpose agencies	56	15 (27%)
Childcare	7	6 (86%)
Learning disability	47	21 (45%)
Total	110	42 (38%)

or the organization did not have a clear responsibility for the care of vulnerable children or people with a learning disability. Six hundred addresses remained from which we randomly selected 110 agencies. The sample included 55 multi-purpose agencies providing services for a wide range of client groups, mainly statutory agencies such as social services departments, and 55 specialist, mainly voluntary sector agencies. Additional information led to one specialist agency being reclassified as multi-purpose (see Table 3.1). Despite several follow-up contacts we were only able to obtain 42 responses. For the purposes of this analysis we treat three of the multi-purpose agencies as specialist child care agencies, as the documentation we received came from the child care department of the agency, and indicated that this department had its own distinctive set of policies and procedures.

The overall response rate was disappointing and it was not clear why agencies did not respond. However, many of the agencies were going through a period of restructuring associated with changes such as local government reorganization. Thus it is important to see the findings of this survey as tentative and exploratory.

We invited each agency to send us documentation which described its aims and objectives plus any documents on risk. The 42 agencies provided 73 batches of documents. Each document was read and all references to general approaches to management and risk management were identified. Each reference was then examined to see how far it could be classified in terms of risk management using the three doctrinal contests discussed in the previous section.

The recognition of risk

An initial analysis of the documentation indicated relatively limited formal recognition of risk. Just under half (19, 45 per cent) of the agencies were classified as having documentation which indicated a high awareness of risk.

The agencies which responded to our initial contact included both multi-purpose and specialist agencies. We anticipated that these agencies would vary in their sensitivity to risk, with multi-purpose agencies being most sensitive, learning disability least sensitive, and childcare in between. This prediction was based on public sensitivity to care and size: multi-purpose agencies are generally larger and therefore more could go wrong. Child care has higher political visibility because of various inquiries and associated media coverage,

Example 3.1:   Risk as hazard

The review should contain accurate information about the hazard, the risk including evidence of the harm that can/has been caused by a particular risk.

There is a strong argument for recording all risks and then eliminating certain risks which are considered to be trivial taking account of any statutory requirements. Regulation 3 states trivial risks may usually be ignored. Managers should beware of eliminating a risk as trivial without consultation.

Responsibility for hazard reviews should be delegated to first line managers while project/department managers should coordinate the outcomes involving directors where a very significant hazard is identified.

Where the source of a hazard is derived from a particular service or response from a resident the key worker should ensure the involvement of that person and others in a review and subsequent assessment. Normally such a review should be first identified in individual planning meetings. The key worker has a responsibility to ensure these activities do not in themselves label, discriminate or cause unnecessary breaches of confidentiality or disrespect to the individual concerned.

If a risk is serious it should be considered separately from the planning meeting while the key worker should continue to ensure the resident is represented in any discussion.

Already at this stage it may be apparent that immediate steps can be taken to eliminate a risk where costs may be low or actions simple. Merely to have reviewed will have raised a heightened awareness of risk. Actions should therefore be recorded and taken. If some risk remains, the process will need to be continued.

and the 1989 Children Act places a clear legal duty on agencies to assess the risk of abuse. However, there was little difference between agencies. Ten of the 21 (48 per cent) agencies specializing in learning disability were classified as risk sensitive, and five of the nine (56 per cent) child care agencies. Only five of the 12 (42 per cent) multi-purpose agencies were classified as risk sensitive.

When the agency did have explicit risk policies, the operating definition of risk in these policies was risk as a danger or hazard which must be identified and countered to ensure the safety of users and others. This is clear in the following extract (Example 3.1) from a learning disability risk policy where risk and hazard are used interchangeably.

In the NHS, concerns with risk were associated with the removal of Crown Immunity and the rise in litigation. As May pointed out, although alleged medical negligence claims have trebled in five years and are set to cost the NHS nearly £150 million in 1996, NHS Trusts do not appear to have responded with the obvious strategy of developing risk management policies:

So what are the ethical solutions to the rising tide of medical litigation? Clearly, effective risk management has a part to play in identifying and avoiding many problems which might otherwise land Trusts in court. Yet there is little research to show how many have adopted structured risk management policies in spite of the NHS Executive's 130-page guidance document, *Risk Management in the NHS*, issued in 1993. The Institute of Risk Management, which carried out an independent survey of Trusts to assess the position, had 71 replies to its questionnaire. Only 34 per cent had a dedicated risk management strategy endorsed by the board, only 26 per cent had full-time risk managers and 52 per cent had risk managers 'of sorts'.

(May 1996: 18–19)

ORGANIZATIONAL CHOICE AND RISK

To examine the ways in which agencies respond to risk, we study each of the three doctrinal contests in turn, first considering each in relationship to the evidence provided by agencies about their general management processes and then in relationship to specific risk management.

Participation in decisions

General
Most agencies (29, 69 per cent) provided some information on the range of participation in general decision making. They generally emphasized the openness of decision making. The majority emphasized their commitment to opening or widening decision making to include non-experts, especially users, in general decision making (22, or 76 per cent of the agencies which discussed this issue). There was a difference between childcare agencies and other agencies. Only half of the specialist child care agencies indicated that they sought to include families in decision making. The majority of multi-purpose agencies and most (13 out of 16) of the agencies providing for people with learning disabilities emphasized the role of lay opinion, especially user involvement in decision making.

Risk specific
Seventeen agencies provided information on the range of participation in risk decision making. The emphasis was on the openness of decision making. Only a small minority of agencies restricted risk decision making to experts (6, or 35 per cent, of the agencies which discussed this issue). The majority emphasized their commitment to opening or widening decision making to include non-expert or lay people, especially service users, in risk decision making. Only one childcare agency indicated that other non-experts were involved in risk decision making. In learning disability agencies and multi-purpose agencies, there was a stronger emphasis on openness and wider participation than in specialist childcare agencies.

Example 3.2: A 'broad participatory' approach to risk management

FAMILY CENTRE CHILD PROTECTION POLICY
As adults and because of the job we do as social workers, our responsibility is
to make sure children are Happy, Cared For and Safe. This will mean that
sometimes in the best interest of the child we will talk to others to get the
help the child needs. Usually we will discuss this with you, the parents and
carers of the children. However, sometimes to protect children we cannot.

To illustrate the difference between the approaches we have selected examples from two policies. The first example (3.2) was taken from the documentation provided by an agency which specialized in providing care for
children. We classified it as broad participation because it emphasized the
importance of consultation with parents in the decision-making process.
However, participation was limited in a number of ways: there was no explicit
reference to the child, his or her advocate or to other lay participants, and the
agency gave primacy to its interpretation of the best interests of the child over
its commitment to consultation, and reserved the right not to consult in
certain circumstances.

The second example (3.3) is also derived from the procedures for making
decisions in relationship to child protection, and is a statement provided by a
National Health Service Trust. There was no reference to wider participation in
decision making, for example through involving service users or any other
non-expert stakeholders. The decision-making process was to take place
within a circle of experts using their judgements. Thus the decision was seen
as one for which professionals were accountable and for which they must take
responsibility. Although this statement is dealing with the early stages of the
decision-making process, which are likely to be more expert-oriented, the
discussion is not set in a wider context which could have brought in wider
participation.

Example 3.3: A 'narrow participatory' approach to risk management

WHENEVER IT IS SUSPECTED THAT A CHILD HAS BEEN ABUSED OR IS IN
DANGER OF SUFFERING SIGNIFICANT HARM THE FOLLOWING STEPS
MUST BE TAKEN:
1 Discuss concerns with a senior colleague, Consultant Paediatrician, Child
   Protection Specialist or Named Nurse Child Protection (Learning
   Disabilities).
2 If the case is already known to Social Services inform the appropriate Social
   Worker. Or if the case is not known to Social Services contact the Customer
   Relations Team or Emergency Duty Team (out of hours).

Example 3.4: A 'learning' policy

1 *Introduction*
Official inquiries into disasters and abuses often show that employees realised someone was in danger but did not raise their concern in time or that if they did it was not heeded by those in charge.

2 *Policy statement*
It is the expectation within (this agency) that all staff are keen to see improvement in the service, are open to new ideas and not afraid to deal with bad practice. This expectation may not always be met and staff may face difficulties when wishing to complain about bad practice. A route will always be available for any staff to voice concerns about any practice issues.

3 *Procedure*
(This agency) has adopted the guidelines enclosed. The guidelines are supplemented by the following information which applies to the four circumstances:
- when the issue applies to a member of staff whom you supervise;
- when the issue applies to a peer colleague;
- when the issue applies to your supervisor;
- when the issue applies to general working practice.

4 *When the issue applies to a member of staff whom you supervise:*
- discuss with the member of staff;
- seek clarification;
- question what they are doing;
- ask how it will help the client;
- keep a written record of the discussion;
- clarify the next step. Options include:
  - resolve via redefinition of . . . goals;
  - involve your line manager;
  - agree you are satisfied by the response.

This should be agreed by normal line management supervision.

5 *When the issue applies to a peer colleague*
- discuss with the colleague;
- clarify the situation;
- ask how it will help the client;
- clarify the next step. Options include:
  - agree you are satisfied with the response;
  - say you must discuss the issue with the line manager of your colleague.

Internal incentive systems

General
Documentation provided less information on the incentive structures than on participation in decision making. Over half the agencies (23, 55 per cent) did

not discuss them. Those agencies that did were relatively evenly balanced between nine agencies, which emphasized the allocation of blame and eight, which emphasized learning. The three childcare agencies which discussed this issue all emphasized the allocation of blame. The multi-purpose agencies and the learning disability agencies tended to emphasize learning.

Risk decision making
Only 13 agencies provided information on the range of participation in risk decision making. Again there was a relatively even balance between agencies adopting a punitive approach (seven agencies) and those emphasizing rewards and learning (six agencies). The three childcare agencies which addressed this issue in their documentation all emphasized negative sanctions, whereas three of the four multi-purpose agencies and three of the seven learning disability agencies emphasized reward and agency learning.

To illustrate the difference between the two approaches, we have selected two policies designed to prevent harm and abuse. The first example (3.4) is taken from the documentation of an agency which specialized in providing care for people with a learning disability. The extract indicates the importance which the agency attached to preventing harm and accidents by learning. The agency encouraged its staff to contribute to the development of agency policy and to voice their concerns, so that the agency could improve its practice. The agency fell short of complete commitment to learning. For example, it did not offer staff who raised concerns guarantees of confidentiality or specific forms of protection from disciplinary action.

The second example (3.5) is taken from the guidelines of a learning disability service and deals with the consumption of alcohol. Whereas clients are permitted to consume alcohol as long as a risk analysis has taken place, staff are not permitted to drink any alcohol while on duty. Although the type of harm which may result is not explicitly identified, any staff found to be drinking while on duty will be disciplined.

Example 3.5: A 'blaming' policy

Living in the Community encompasses community presence, participation and choice. All tenants have the right to express a choice as to whether they do or do not wish to drink alcoholic beverages . . . All clients will have a considered alcohol amount stated within their care plan/risk analysis . . .
All care staff owe a duty of care to clients which cannot be safely exercised when alcohol has been consumed . . .
staff must be aware that drinking amounts of alcohol prior to commencing duty may affect their work performance to an adverse extent, and adversely influence their duty of care and put the clients at risk . . .
Any staff found drinking alcohol whilst on duty will be subject to the Trust Disciplinary Procedure.

Managing the external environment

General
A substantial minority of agencies (17, 40 per cent) did not discuss the ways in which they managed the environment. Those agencies which did discuss this tended to emphasize rapid response to situations (13 agencies) rather than seeking to identify potential problems (nine agencies). Three agencies indicated that they anticipated some types of problems and responded to others. None of the specialist childcare agencies sought to anticipate problems. Four such agencies indicated that they responded rapidly, although one childcare agency indicated that it anticipated some types of problems and responded to others. Those multi-purpose agencies which provided information were evenly divided between anticipating and responding. Among specialist learning disability agencies there was a greater emphasis on identifying potential problems (seven agencies), though two agencies emphasized rapid response and two response plus anticipation.

Risk decision making
Eighteen agencies provided information on the ways in which they managed environmental risk. Nine agencies emphasized rapid response to dangerous situations and six sought to identify potential hazards. Three agencies indicated that they anticipated some types of hazards and responded to others. Three of the specialist childcare agencies sought to respond rapidly and one indicated that it anticipated some types of hazards and responded to others. Multi-purpose agencies were evenly balanced between agencies which anticipated and those which responded. Among learning disability agencies there was again a greater emphasis on anticipating risk (seven agencies) than on rapid response (three agencies).

The first of the two policy examples (3.6) is taken from the documentation provided by one agency which specialized in providing care for people with a learning disability. We classified it as a risk anticipation as there was a strong emphasis on using reviews to identify potential hazards.

Example 3.6: An 'anticipatory' policy

It is the responsibility of each director to make sure hazard reviews take place. Each manager should complete reviews within their area of control. These reviews should cover:
- risks in the *workplace;*
- risks encountered in *particular work activities;*
- risks associated with *care of a particular resident* (a resident should not be seen as a hazard. The source hazard should be identified);
- risks which can arise from *the manner in which a particular service is conducted.*

Example 3.7: A 'rapid response' policy

If you suspect any kind of abuse or neglect you must report it to the school's Child Protection Co-ordinator or a senior member of staff. Many people are hesitant about doing this because of the implications – if they are only voicing vague suspicions they do not want to be responsible for the Police, Social Services, etc., being brought in and commencing a full scale investigation. The fear of seriously damaging relationships with children and their parents, particularly if suspicions eventually prove to be unfounded, is a very strong deterrent to reporting incidents. You may feel that you could be instrumental in children being removed from their families and afterwards you may have far more contact with very angry parents than, say, the social worker, doctor or policeman.

It is quite understandable that you should have these fears but the decision to take a case forward is not yours to make. Your only responsibility is to report your suspicions – the Child Protection Co-ordinator will then decide what, if any, further action will be taken. If a case is formally investigated there will inevitably be at least one case conference to pull together all the agencies and disciplines who will have information and direct knowledge of the child and/or the family.

If you originally reported the suspected abuse you may be requested to attend. It is important that you keep accurate records at the time of reporting the abuse so that you can be sure of your facts and make a positive and confident contribution to the conference.

A copy of the relevant section of ' – Child Protection Committee's Child Abuse Guidelines and Procedures' is reproduced at the end of this booklet for information.

ALL YOU NEED TO DO IF YOU SUSPECT ANY SORT OF ABUSE IS TO REPORT IT TO THE CHILD PROTECTION CO-ORDINATOR OR SENIOR MEMBER OF STAFF

The second example (3.7) illustrates the alternative approach based on rapid response and is derived from documentation provided by a school. The emphasis is on identifying harmful situations and ensuring that they are investigated as rapidly as possible.

Comment
The low overall response rate (38 per cent) and small numbers of agencies answering some questions must be borne in mind. Our analysis of documentation shows variations in the ways in which welfare agencies respond to risk. Some agencies are highly aware and sensitive to risk but generally both awareness and sensitivity are limited with few agencies having well-developed risk management strategies. There were variations in the strategies which agencies used both in general management and in the management of risk. The strategies varied both in terms of specific areas of management and in

Table 3.2: Overall approaches to risk and decision making

	Agencies			
	Childcare	Learning disability	Multi-purpose	All
Sensitive to risk	5/9 (56%)	10/21 (48%)	5/12 (42%)	20/42 (48%)
Broad participation in decision making	3/6 (50%)	13/16 (81%)	6/7 (86%)	22/29 (76%)
Non-blaming approach	0/3 (0%)	5/8 (62%)	3/6 (50%)	8/17 (48%)
Anticipation	1/5 (20%)	9/11 (82%)	2/9 (22%)	12/25 (48%)

Note: Entry for each cell is number of positives and total response given as number and percentage.

terms of specific types of organizations. Generally, then, agencies were most open in terms of participation in decision making. However, this tended to be through the involvement of users rather than wider lay involvement in decision making. They tended to be most defensive in relationship to the management of the environment, but were more evenly divided in their use of negative and positive sanctions for internal management. There was also a difference between the different types of agencies; childcare agencies were the most defensive, while agencies specializing in providing services for people with a learning disability tended to be the most open with multi-purpose agencies in between. Learning disability agencies tended to have broader participation in decision making, to emphasize organizational learning rather than blaming and to anticipate risk (see Table 3.2).

CONCLUSION

Our analysis has focused mainly on the issue of how organizations respond to risk. It has not addressed the wider issue of why organizations adopt different strategies for managing risk. It is possible to adopt a crude functionalism to this question and suggest that different types of organizations have different types of functions and that risk sensitivity is related to organizational function. Yet as Douglas (1992) pointed out in her discussion of Perrow's concept of a normal accident, two organizations performing the same function may have quite different ways of managing risk:

> Institutions could be graded quite objectively as safety ensuring systems. Charles Perrow's analysis of 'normal accidents' is a step in this direction. But he did not focus on the 'human factor', either at the individual, or the level of institutional authority. He concentrated on an industrial typology. Two institutions in the same industry, handling the same materials, dealing in the same markets, can have quite different blaming patterns, for example, two universities, two publishers, two boatyards, two docks.
>
> (Douglas 1992: 12–13)

Using cultural theory, Douglas argued that the ways in which organizations respond to risk, and, in particular, allocate responsibility when accidents or catastrophes occur, relate to an organization's overall sense of security. For example, organizations, in the sense of a group of people with a common purpose, can see themselves as under attack if the continued existence of the organization or group is threatened through the loss of members. One response to this type of threat is to seek to retain members and control by establishing or reinforcing boundaries. This can be done by creating clearly defined systems which either externalize blame or allocate it to marginal individuals within the organization, i.e. scapegoating.

Our data tends to confirm Douglas's prediction that agency response to this turbulence is not likely to be uniform and is likely to be mediated by the existing structures and management of the agency. Thus agencies vary in their perception of and response to this turbulence and their confidence in their ability to predict risks. In Chapter 4 we extend our analysis by considering the impact of informal relations within agencies on the management of risk.

4

THE INFLUENCE OF INFORMAL RELATIONS ON THE MANAGEMENT OF RISK

Larry Harrison, Andy Alaszewski and Mike Walsh

In Chapter 3, we examined the formal or public response of welfare agencies to risk. In this chapter we develop the analysis by considering the influence of the informal relations within organizations on risk management. In the first section, we discuss the general nature and significance of the informal structure of organizations. In the second section, we draw upon evidence from a study of welfare agencies to explore whether there is a divergence between the formal and informal accounts of risk management strategies. Finally, in the third section, we consider the actual practices adopted by front-line workers and managers and their implications for the management of risk in welfare agencies.

THE IMPORTANCE OF INFORMAL RELATIONS WITHIN AGENCIES

The limits of Weberian analysis

In Chapter 3, we used Weber as the starting point for our analysis of organizations and the ways in which they manage risk. Although this approach provides an important insight into the nature of organizations, especially bureaucracies, in contemporary society, it has important limitations. Weber concentrated on the formal aspects of organizations, i.e. their public statements of aims, and their formal structure of rules and procedures. As these public statements tend to be made by the most senior personnel in organizations, they represent only one view or version of the way in which the organizations operate. Although these ideal types purport to describe the reality of organizations and the ways in which they operate, they also serve to justify and legitimate the claims of dominant groups within these organizations. The Weberian organization is one in which leadership is provided by either bureaucratic superiors or charismatic leaders who exercise authority over their subordinates, and the aims and objectives of the organization are equated with the aims and objectives of its leaders. As Giddens argued:

> Weber's analysis of bureaucracy gives prime place to formal relations within organizations. The more bureaucratized an organization is, in Weber's terms, the more tasks are fixed and detailed. He has little to say about the informal connections and small-group relations that exist in all organizations.
>
> (Giddens 1993: 289)

Thus the public statements made by organizations should not necessarily be taken at face value. As McKinley indicated:

> Increasingly, skepticism is being voiced concerning the professed activity of certain formal organizations. There is a body of evidence accumulating which suggests that organizations seldom accomplish what their formal charter and the claims of administrators or representatives suggest.
>
> (McKinley 1975: 344)

Studies that have examined how power is actually exercised within organizations show the limitations of the Weberian approach. These studies have identified informal structures within organizations. Groups lower down the organization often do not share the aims of senior personnel. These groups can exercise a considerable degree of control over their own work and use this control to pursue goals that are different to the formal and stated public goals of the organization. The formal structure of authority does not reflect the reality of the struggle for power within many organizations. Workers at the front line seek control over their work and may develop considerable power as they do the job. They often are the main sources of information about how the organization discharges its responsibility and their actions may be difficult to observe and therefore to control. Indeed, Beynon (1973: 140–1) found that front-line workers use illegitimate means such as sabotage to control their working environment. As McKinley pointed out:

> it appears, from considerable field research, that in reality formal organizations are influenced (perhaps even controlled) from the bottom, as well as, or instead of, from the top. Certainly, it seems that both inmates or clients and lower employees within formal organizations wield considerable power and influence not associated with their formally defined position. Such participants may be said to have informal personal power, but little formal authority.
>
> (1975: 349)

Human relations

The importance of informal relations was first noted by industrial psychologists studying the influence of the working environment on productivity. During the 1930s, a group of researchers from the University of Chicago undertook a series of experiments in the Bank Wiring Room at the Western

Electric Company industrial plant in Hawthorne (see Roethlisberger and Dickson 1939). The researchers identified a paradoxical effect. Their experiments involved changing working conditions, for example by altering the lighting within the workplace. They anticipated that improvements in working conditions would result in improvements in productivity. Their initial experiments confirmed this hypothesis; they found production increased when they improved the working conditions. However, they decided to test the results by making the working conditions worse. It was found that this also increased productivity.

In the social science literature, these findings are now referred to as the 'Hawthorne Effect'. The research team investigated the reasons for this. Within the factory, the research team identified informal groups which effectively controlled the level of output. Informal leaders in these groups decided what the reasonable output or rate was. This norm could be achieved by all members of the group not just the most skilled. Any individual who exceeded the norm, or 'rate-busted' was effectively challenging the informal leaders so was subject to strong group pressure to conform, for example they were ostracized. The informal group played a crucial role in the 'Hawthorne Effect'. The informal leaders of the work group were flattered by the attention of the research team and wanted to please them, therefore they had allowed the group to increase production when the researchers changed the working conditions both positively and negatively.

This 'bottom-up' approach to organizations has led to a variety of research. Some of this research is radical as it aims to empower workers. For example, Beynon in his study of the Ford's Halewood plant described his study in the following way:

> I have told the story of other people's experiences, some of which I shared, as an outsider. An outsider who was accepted inside. These pages . . . are made up of the activity and conversation of men and women in the pub, the factory, on the picket-line or in their homes, combined in an attempt to describe the lives that people lead when they work on the shop floor of a large car factory; to outline the crises they encounter and the way in which they try to make sense of them and the world they live in . . . the book is written in the hope that they, and others like them, will be able to identify parts of themselves in the story and perhaps, thereby, see more clearly the way they are going.
>
> (Beynon 1973: 9)

Most of the research is more traditional. It recognizes the role which informal groups and leaders can play, and sees them as a potential way of enhancing the efficiency of organizations. For example, Blau, in his study of a government agency, examined the operation of agents who investigated potential violation of regulations. The formal rules of the agency specified that if agents had a problem and needed assistance then they should consult their supervisors. However, Blau found that agents avoided consulting their supervisors because they feared it would affect their rating. Instead, there was informal consultation between agents which:

transformed an aggregate of individuals who happened to have the same supervisor into a cohesive group . . . this practice contributed to operating efficiency, because it improved the quality of the decisions of agents. Every agent knew he could obtain help with solving problems whenever he needed it.

(Blau 1963: 135; see also Blau and Meyer 1971: 38–50)

This approach formed the basis for a major area of interdisciplinary study, Human Relations. Researchers operating within the Human Relations framework are interested in the empirical study of organization, especially organizations involved in industrial production mainly in Western countries. In a classic study of coal mining, Trist and colleagues (1963) identified two types of activities and two types of boundaries within the mine – activities which related to the overt task of digging coal, which they referred to as 'task activities', and the divisions between such activities, which were 'task boundaries'. They contrasted these to activities required to maintain relations between individuals and groups, such as creating and maintaining work teams, which were associated with social or sentient boundaries.

Trist and colleagues argued that a failure to recognize informal group relations led to organizational inefficiency. There was a tendency for informal groups to form within task areas, i.e. for a specific function to be given to a group and for tasks and sentient boundaries to coincide. They argued that this was dysfunctional as groups focused on their own task and not the overall achievement of organizational goals. Such specialized task-based groups tended to compete with and blame other groups when things went wrong and did not seek to cooperate to solve problems. They argued that the organization should be engineered so that groups performed a range of activities and took responsibility for integrating these activities and for the overall achievement of organizational goals. This work has led to moves to job enrichment and to experiments in factories with informal groups being given autonomy, as on Volvo production lines.

Researchers working in the Weberian and Human Relations traditions see themselves as independent observers and analysts who stand outside organizations and seek to understand how they work. The Weberian approach tends to accept formal public statements as the key defining element of organizations and is therefore fundamentally conservative, accepting the claims of senior personnel about the nature of power and decision making. The Human Relations approach is potentially more radical, accepting that formal structures may at best be only part of the story and that lower ranking employees have their own views about the purpose of the organizations and also the power to act independently.

Since much of the literature on organizations is based on work in either industrial organizations or public bureaucracies, in the next section we will focus specifically on the literature on the informal aspects of care agencies to examine whether similar themes exist.

Health and welfare agencies

In the study of welfare organizations, it is possible to identify a similar interest in, and awareness of, the difference between formal and informal structures. However there is one major difference, which can be illustrated by considering the 'bottom-up' perspective. In industrial organizations the 'bottom-up' perspective emphasizes the role and importance of operatives such as assembly line workers or coal miners. In the study of welfare organizations, especially organizations which provide care and/or treatment within a residential setting, there are actually two potentially disempowered groups, front-line workers and service users. In research in welfare agencies, the emphasis has often been on the service users' perspective. For example, in Goffman's classic study of the Asylum he concentrated mainly on 'instrumental formal organizations' which he defined as: 'a system of purposely coordinated activities designed to produce some over-all explicit ends' (Goffman 1961: 161). However, a central interest of Goffman's was the ways in which service users, or in his terms 'inmates', resist and defy the formal culture of the asylum as expressed in its rules and norms, through a counter culture which forms the hidden underlife of the institution. He summarizes his findings in the following way:

> In every social establishment, there are official expectations as to what the participant owes the establishment . . . Whenever we look at a social establishment, we find a counter to this theme: we find that participants decline in some way to accept the official view of what they they should be putting into and getting out of the organization and, behind this, of what sort of self and world they are to accept for themselves. Where enthusiasm is expected, there will be apathy; where loyalty, there will be disaffection . . . Whenever worlds are laid on, underlives develop.
>
> (Goffman 1961: 267)

Belknap, in his study of an American State Mental Hospital, also identified a difference between the formal and public structure of the organization and its internal informal structure, but he saw the difference in terms of the objectives and power of different groups of staff rather than residents. In the formal structure authority and power were located with trained professional staff in a 'medical-psychiatric' system, i.e. the clinical director and his professional staff of doctors, nurses, social workers, etc. The overt and official aim of the hospital was to treat the patients to enable them to return to society, the reality was very different. There was a parallel 'custodial-maintenance' system dominated by untrained but well-established staff, such as business managers and ward attendants, which controlled decision making in the hospital. In this system the aims were very different, they were to maintain control and order in the hospital and at the same time to minimize cost and maximize production by efficiently exploiting inmate labour. It was anti-therapeutic, as patients were assessed on the basis of the utility of labour not their therapeutic potential.

The informal culture of the institution was created and maintained by a core of interconnected families from which the majority of attendants were recruited. These families were the informal leaders and used their position to undermine the medical-psychiatric system and to impose their own order on the wards:

> The main function of the informal organization on wards is to set up a system which permits him (the attendant) to adjust personally the requirements of psychiatric treatment, as represented by the hospital's formal classification on the one hand, with the requirements of daily patient management on the other . . . These patterns are justified by an ideology centering around the attendant's functions in the hospital, and the entire system is held together with considerable solidarity, or in-group feeling, against patients and the professionals, who are out-groups.
>
> (Belknap 1956: 151)

Although Belknap does not explicitly discuss the two systems in terms of risk, it is clear that they had very different implications for risk management. In the formal public system, the hospital was a therapeutic organization designed to effectively assess and manage risk, balancing community and individual interests. The hospital claimed to admit individuals who were a danger to themselves and others, place them in a safe and protected environment and provide treatment to enable them to return safely to the community. In reality, Belknap found there was no proper assessment at admission, and the institution admitted a variety of people with varying needs, not just people with mental illness but also people with learning disabilities and people who were unable to support themselves. In practice, the hospital was concerned with minimizing any danger to the public and achieved this by exploiting inmates and effectively subjecting them to abuse.

Miller and Gwynne (1972), in their study of residential institutions for young physically disabled people, recognized the importance of formal and informal structures. For example, in one Cheshire Home Unit (Le Court), they found two separate structures with different definitions of the main purpose of the home, a formal 'top-down' structure designed to provide 'care' for dependent residents and an informal resident-led structure which saw the prime function of the unit as developmental, i.e. enhancing capacities and autonomy of its residents:

> we could identify two separate organizations in Le Court, each acting on the assumption that the other was jeopardizing the real purpose of the institution. The formal organization was along hierarchical lines. The trustees of the Cheshire Foundation delegated authority to the Management Committee, which in turn delegated responsibility for the day-to-day running of the home to the warden . . . Such an organization, while tailored to effective performance of the task of care, made little allowance for the development task. This latter task had over the years become firmly vested in an informal organization of residents whose voice was the Residents' Welfare Committee. There was no staff leadership for this task.
>
> (Miller and Gwynne 1972: 34–5)

This split between formal and informal created stress and was dysfunctional. The warden was on the interface of the two structures and acted as a scapegoat when tensions between the two structures and two sets of purposes undermined the public aim of creating 'a happy home' (Miller and Gwynne 1972: 36).

Although Miller and Gwynne did not use a risk framework in their analysis, it is clear that the tensions between the formal and the informal structures could be understood in such a framework. The formal structure was concerned with creating a minimum risk environment thus minimizing potential harm to residents. Miller and Gwynne refered to this as the warehousing model of care. The residents wanted a more stimulating and riskier environment to provide stimulation and interest. Miller and Gwynne labelled this as the horticultural model of care. The warden had the impossible task of reconciling these conflicting models of care and risk assessment and management.

Miller and Gwynne worked within a human relations framework but they used a systems approach as the basis of their comparative analysis of Cheshire Homes. The human relations approach to organizations can be seen as an early strand of systems thinking (e.g. Jackson 1991). Hard systems approaches see organizations as objective entities with characteristics that can be measured and compared. Indeed, some early theorists such as Parsons (1951: 3) argued that organizations could be studied in the same way as biological systems, i.e. they had an internal structure which rather than being hard and soft tissues of the body were institutionalized patterns of roles and relationships.

From a systems perspective, the organizational goal of the homes could be seen as assisting disabled people to die. This is clear in Miller and Gwynne's critique of both the warehousing and the horticultural model:

> What both models neglect and deny is that, if we are correct in our interpretation that by the very fact of committing people to institutions of this type, society is defining them as, in effect, socially dead, then the essential task to be carried out is to help the inmates to make their transition from social to physical death.
>
> (1972: 88)

This negative analysis indicated that there were some serious difficulties in applying this type of system approach to welfare agencies. In such organizations, purpose and power were especially problematic and contested concepts. Formal authority was often divided between senior managers and senior professionals, such as doctors, and informal power was exercised not just by lower employees but also by service users.

One way out of this quandary is to follow a 'soft' system approach and examine the organizations in terms of the variety of groups involved, the different interests and aims of these groups and the extent to which the organizations meet the interests of different groups of participants. During the 1980s, 'hard' systems thinking was increasingly challenged by 'soft' systems. Soft systems approaches suggest that hard objective measurable reality is an illusion, and that a way of thinking about organizations has become confused with the nature of organizations. The soft systems approach retains a concern with organizations as holistic units, but is interested in the different ways in which these units are conceptually constructed and perceived and form parts of cognitive systems (see Jackson 1991: 4–7; see also Checkland 1981).

This approach to organizations underlies Smith and Cantley's (1985) 'pluralistic evaluation' of a psycho-geriatric day hospital. Although Smith and Cantley derived their theoretical framework from political science rather than systems theory, there are strong similarities in the two approaches. The aim of Smith and Cantley's approach was to be 'independent and neutral' (p. 14) by taking into account the variety of groups and their interests (though not the users' perspective). They sought to overcome the limitations of research which examined the formal aspects of organizations as this merely indicated that 'most organizations fail to live up to their utopian ideals' (p. 13) and did not explain how and why these failures occur. Their approach was based on a detailed case ethnography which sought to identify different groups and their criteria of success:

> if we are to understand and evaluate the part played by several different groups involved in the care of a client group then we must understand how they use different criteria of success in their own interests and how 'success' thus operates in the social context of its use.
>
> (Smith and Cantley 1985: 12)

This approach can be applied to study ways in which welfare organizations manage risk. In particular to contrast formal organizational risk management strategies with key participants' perceptions of the nature of risk and how it can be managed. We will discuss the findings of such a study in the next section.

Comment
Although the formal structures of organizations are important, as they define the public position of the organization and provide the framework for internal decision making, it is also necessary to study the informal structures, as the reality of decision making may be very different. Indeed, in traditional welfare agencies, such as mental hospitals, the formal structure in some organizations may be seen as a smoke screen that insulates the informal structure from external scrutiny and change. In the remainder of this chapter we examine the relationship between formal and informal structures for the assessment and management of risk in a sample of welfare agencies.

FORMAL STRUCTURES AND INFORMAL RELATIONS: A COMPARATIVE STUDY

In the remainder of this chapter we will use evidence from a study of welfare agencies to explore the relationship between formal and informal accounts of risk management practices and procedures. In the first part, we will describe how we collected the data which forms the basis for our discussion.

Table 4.1: Sample of agencies

	Specialist		Multi-purpose
	Child protection	Learning disability	
Agencies with risk policies	2	2	5
Agencies without risk policies	2	1	3

Studying the relationship between formal structures and informal relations

In Chapter 3, we described how we examined the formal aspects of agencies' response to risk by undertaking a survey of welfare agencies in one English health region. This study showed some differences between agencies in terms of their sensitivity to risk and in terms of their general management and risk management styles. To examine the impact of formal structures, we selected 15 agencies for more intensive study (see Table 4.1). They were divided into seven specialist and eight generic or multi-purpose agencies.

In each of the 15 agencies, the research team collected data on risk management using interviews and questionnaires. The research team aimed to interview five staff from each agency: one senior manager, two middle managers and two front-line workers. Thus the target was 75 interviews, of which 61 were undertaken (81 per cent). For the questionnaires, the research team also wanted a sample of managers and front-line workers. Given variations in the size and structure of the agencies, it was decided to invite all agency staff to participate. Again, because of the size of the agencies the sample varied, from one respondent to 44. A total of 160 questionnaires were returned, which represents a response rate of 63 per cent. Since the main focus of the study was on the relationship between formal and informal aspects of risk management, we over-sampled those agencies which claimed to have policies for the management of risk (129 respondents or 81 per cent of the sample were from agencies with policies). The same bias was also evident in the interviews (42 or 69 per cent).

Employee perceptions of agency policy

In Chapter 3, we classified organizations in terms of: their *sensitivity* to risk issues; the degree of *participation* in decision making; their kinds of internal incentive systems (*accountability*); and their strategies for anticipating or reacting to risk (*environment*). This was based on a review of their official statements and policy documents. The first step of our analysis was to examine how and in what ways formal statements about agency policy were reflected in individual employees' understanding of risk management within the agency. In both our interviews and our questionnaire survey of managers and workers,

Table 4.2: Congruence: number and percentage of respondents agreeing with agency's formal position

	Managers agreeing		Workers agreeing		All	
	Number	(%)	Number	(%)	Number	(%)
Sensitivity	25	45	60	37	85	39
Accountability	9	*	22	42	28	45
Environment	14	41	47	52	61	49
Participation	16	29	66	41	82	38

Note: *insufficient numbers of classified documents to present congruence as percentage

we checked this by asking a series of questions designed to explore employees' perceptions of the actual strategies adopted by their agency. We were concerned with the fit or congruence between agency and employee accounts, in other words if agency statements indicated that the agency adopted a blameist style of management, then employees who stated that the agency was blameist were classified as congruent and those who did not were non-congruent.

When the results of the interviews and questionnaires were combined we had a total sample of 217 employees: 55 managers and 162 workers. Table 4.2 shows that, in almost every case, only a minority of employees agreed that the formal description of their agency reflected organizational practice. There was little difference between managers and workers in this perception, except on the questions concerning participation and environment, where workers were rather more likely than managers to agree with their organization's documented position. Even here, however, those who agreed with the formal position on participation were outnumbered by those who did not.

Only on the question of 'environment' did a small majority of workers (52 per cent) agree with their agency's formal position. When the analysis was restricted to those who demonstrated knowledge of their agency's policies, the percentage of congruent workers remained unchanged, but the levels of congruence went down in all other cases. Thus, only 34 per cent of managers and 30 per cent of workers agreed with their agency's position on risk sensitivity among those who claimed to know their agency's policy. This suggests that better informed employees were more rather than less critical. Overall, there was a divergence between the formal and informal aspects of risk management within most agencies.

OFFICIAL POLICY AND PRACTITIONER AUTONOMY

It is clear, from the evidence presented above, that there was a large discrepancy between employee perceptions and official accounts of policy. We explored a number of factors which might affect the congruence between formal and informal accounts, including the degree of bureaucratization within the agency; the influence of agency status as a statutory or non-statutory agency; and the nature of the agencies' task, i.e. the differences between specialist and generic or multi-purpose agencies.

Bureaucracy: mechanistic and organic management styles

From the detailed interviews which we conducted within the 15 agencies, it appears that employees were more likely to agree with the formal account of risk management if the organization's style could be characterized as mechanistic rather than organic, in Burns and Stalker's (1961) terms. It was the organizations that both possessed explicit risk management policies, documented a policy of wide participation in decision making and a non-punitive management style, and which attempted to anticipate rather than react to risky situations, where there was most likely to be dissonance between the formal and informal accounts. Thus, 68 per cent (24) of respondents from one organization that had an explicit policy of treating mistakes as learning opportunities did not believe that this was how the organization operated in practice, compared to 37 per cent of respondents in the four agencies that had an unequivocal policy of holding members of staff accountable for the consequences of their decisions.

Although these differences were most pronounced in organizations that attempted to depart from more conventional management styles, there was not a single organization in which there was unanimity; opinion was divided among both managers and workers over the nature of their organizations. It appears that there were large differences in the way in which the same organizations were perceived by those who worked within them.

Agency status

When the interview and questionnaire samples are combined, there appears to be little difference between respondents in the statutory and non-statutory sectors in terms of their agreement with their agencies' formal position on risk sensitivity, accountability and participation. We found that respondents from the statutory sector were marginally more likely to agree with their agency's stated strategy on the environment, i.e. whether the agency anticipated or reacted to risk. Fifty-three per cent of respondents in the statutory sector were congruent compared to 46 per cent in the non-statutory sector. However, this may reflect the difficulty we experienced in classifying policy documents on this dimension. Only seven of the 15 agencies provided documents which could be classified in terms of anticipation or resiliance. When disaggregated, only one of these agencies claimed to have a strategy of reacting to risk, while five claimed to adopt an anticipationist stance, and one claimed to do both. All respondents were congruent in the one (statutory) agency which described a reactive policy, while there was no support from the staff for the position of the one (non-statutory) agency which declared a strategy of both anticipating and reacting. The range of congruence for the remaining five agencies was from 10 per cent to 69 per cent (both of these extreme values were from non-statutory agencies). Overall, therefore, whether the agency was located in the

Table 4.3: Congruence: number and percentage of respondents agreeing with agency's formal position by agency task

| | Congruent employees | | | | | |
| | Child protection | | Learning disability | | Multi-purpose | |
	Number	(%)	Number	(%)	Number	(%)
Sensitivity	11	35	28	39	48	40
Participation	10	32	24	35	48	41

statutory or non-statutory sector did not seem to influence respondents unduly.

Agency task

Table 4.3 indicates that, when the interview and questionnaire samples are combined, there is little difference between employees in child protection, learning disability and multi-purpose agencies in terms of their endorsement of agency policies on risk sensitivity. The findings for accountability and environment were distorted by the fact that documentation from only one child protection agency could be classified on these two dimensions: in both cases the overwhelming majority of respondents were incongruent. Where participation was concerned, respondents in multi-purpose agencies were marginally more likely to be congruent than those in child protection and learning disabilities agencies. On this evidence, the agency task does not seem to be a major influence on congruence between the formal and informal accounts of policy, although there is a suggestion that the child protection agencies receive the least confirmation from employees for their official position.

INFORMAL RELATIONS AND RISK

Since the informal aspect of agencies concerns the actual practices of employees, rather than the formal statements or claims about the ways in which decisions are made, the interviews explored specific risk incidents and the ways in which they were managed. We invited each respondent to identify two specific risky situations during the previous six months in which he or she had to make a decision. In the interviews we asked respondents to: 'try to give one example each of any situations in the last six months that have been threatening or potentially rewarding.' If the respondent asked for clarification of 'threat' or 'reward' then the terms 'gains' and 'losses' were used and examples were given if requested, based on a list of general statements of positive and negative consequences. Only one interviewee was unable to answer this (and subsequent) question(s) claiming that she did not understand it since all her decisions were made according to a strict and invariant medical model.

Respondents identified a variety of situations, which were differentiated in terms of the nature of the risk, the probability that it would occur and the perceived consequences. One way of differentiating situations was between decisions that used 'common sense' negative definitions of risk, and were therefore concerned with potential losses and harm, and those which used a more balanced definition and were concerned with positive consequences.

The 60 respondents identified 108 situations. Fifty involved both gains and losses, 32 primarily losses and 26 primarily gains. Despite being prompted to consider situations with positive consequences, therefore, respondents appeared to find it easier to think in terms of loss. The situations involving losses tended to focus on the identification and management of specific hazards, as in the following examples.

Example 4.1: Team manager in social services child assessment team

A death threat was made against me by a client who also posed a security threat to the building. I discussed it with my boss, other managers and the police in order to get protection for the building and me.

Example 4.2: Unit leader in early years team

A family is dominated by domestic violence with all three children being victimised. [The] partner physically assaulted the mother. The children were emotionally damaged. The family was in danger of breaking up. We arranged for the mother [enabled her to decide] and children to go into a refuge. A temporary room – but they were in for three months. The parenting issues seem very secondary in this situation. The mother eventually moved into a house.

The positive situation tended to focus on ways in which the agency could enhance its services, as in the following examples.

Example 4.3: Social worker, team leader in a child protection team

In the management of the team over the year we have had team days where we can discuss issues without interruption. One issue raised is the need for the team to find a structure to maintain output with chaos prevailing . . . this will protect staff. An investigation team is inherently unpredictable work, for example we might face a massive influx of situations. How do you handle the tension between the need to respond quickly and yet have the space to plan – especially in a department that is expected to run?

Example 4.4: Youth court service manager

The environment in [the local prison] is unsatisfactory for young offenders so we established community links with the prison, including visiting facilities; we sent someone in as a troubleshooter to go and observe the regime; we agreed with the prison to set up a post, joint-financed between the health authorities, the prison and social services. This risks setting the precedent that it is all right to have young people in jail, but we argue that the post holder is trying to get young people out – and is being successful.

The situations also varied in their urgency. Most of the examples (93, 86 per cent) given by interviewees related to routine or non-critical decisions. However, 14 per cent (15) related to critical situations, i.e. those with potentially serious consequences. Routine situations tended to have lower perceived consequences and more time in which to make decisions, whereas in critical situations there was often a high probability of harm occurring, combined with a short time-scale for making decisions. Example 4.5 identifies the key features of a routine decision and Example 4.6 those of a critical decision.

Example 4.5: A routine decision

- *Agency* – Specialist learning disability agency; risk policy for assessing client risk.
- *Context* – One of five clients in a community residential unit exhibiting challenging behaviour.
- *Risk* – To other residents; possible consequence, harm to one or more clients; probability medium; time scale not urgent.
- *Decision* – No immediate action, situation monitored.

Example 4.6: A critical decision

- *Agency* – Multi-purpose agency, NHS Community Trust; risk insensitive.
- *Context* – Child protection, visit by community nurse to drug-misusing parents of child who is excluded from school. During visit one of the parents has a needlestick injury and nurse is covered in blood.
- *Risk* – Initially, to the child; possible consequence of continued exclusion from school; probability high; time scale not urgent.
- *Risk* – Subsequently, to the employee and family; consequence possible HIV infection; probability, medium to low; time scale, urgent.
- *Decision* – Immediate action taken by nurse to take family to Accident and Emergency Department. This action contravened agency policy, as nurse should have ensured her own safety. However, subsequent action did fall within policy: following the emergency, the nurse had an HIV test.

Urgency and a high level of harm also underlie the following critical situation:

Example 4.7: Care officer in a unit for people with learning disability

She [the resident] could have gone through the gate, having got into the garden, and injured herself. I would have restrained her but I didn't know where the line was drawn. I was alone in the lounge. She was present voluntarily, without restrictions. I was wanting to persuade her to stay in because she was in danger.

When the respondents had identified risk situations, we asked them a series of questions to explore the ways in which they managed risk. These questions dealt with:

- whether policy had been followed;
- how accountability could be or was exercised in the situation;
- who participated in the main decisions and how influential they were;
- to what extent the agency's environment influenced policy and practice.

Managing risk: following policy

Of the 108 situations identified, respondents discussed their use of agency policy in 100 situations. Of these 100 situations, there was nearly an even division between situations in which policy was followed and situations in which it was not. There was no difference between the employees of agencies which had been categorized as risk sensitive, on the basis of their policy documents, and those rated risk insensitive: the employees of both groups were equally likely to dispense with policy guidance.

We examined why respondents did not follow organizational policies. Part of the explanation related to the nature of the decision and part to the employee's relationship with the agency. In terms of the nature of the decision, there were two main factors: either the respondents did not feel that the policy was relevant to the situation, or the situation presented a dilemma which organizational policies were unable to resolve, so the front-line worker or manager had to exercise professional judgement. Not utilizing policy did not necessarily mean that employees were ignorant of agency policies or insensitive to risk issues.

In the following example, a decision was made not to break into a barricaded room and restrain a resident, although there was a risk that he would injure himself.

Example 4.8: Self-mutilation

We have a client with a history of self harm and suicide attempts. He used to lock himself in his room by putting a chair against the door and then he would cut himself. He was a risk to himself, but also a risk to others: his fellow residents became distressed. We found that intervention escalated things, so I suggested withdrawing next time. Shortly afterwards he [barricaded himself in his room and] was breaking windows . . . My decision was to 'back out'; to 'give him some space.' Simultaneously, I contacted the fire brigade to make sure they had the equipment to get in quick if necessary. Eventually, it was resolved because he allowed someone in to talk.

The next example also illustrates the way in which a practitioner felt that she had to use professional judgement to resolve a dilemma over risk, as the agencies' policies did not provide clear guidance.

Example 4.9: Reporting a suicide attempt

(In a hospital trust, a health visitor who was involved in child protection faced a critical incident with a child in the Accident and Emergency Department. The child had taken a drugs overdose and initially the health visitor found it difficult to identify the range of consequences of the incident.) There were simply vague and uncorroborated bits of information that the boy's family were in legal proceedings with social services, that he had previously been abused and his brother had committed suicide. I was not sure whether I should inform social services or not. If the information was given to social services then they could initiate an investigation. I did not have any power to keep the child in the Accident and Emergency Department and I felt that there was a strong possibility that if I followed the policy guidelines and informed social services, [the child] would immediately leave the hospital and make a further suicide attempt. There was clearly a risk of serious harm to the child and it was not clear which course of action would reduce the risk. I decided to inform social services.

She saw this as a decision based on professional judgement aimed at mini-mizing harm to the child. She felt that the child's history demanded action, even though there were no 'facts'. However, she was also influenced by concern for her own professional well-being and the credibility of the agency. The decision was a 'safety first' action made from a position of personal insecurity.

Managing risk: accountability
In terms of employees' relationship with their agency, a central issue was the respondents' perception of vulnerability or personal insecurity, especially the

Table 4.4: Allocation of blame

Liable to be blamed	Percentage of risk situations (N = 60) (%)
No one	22
Respondent	10
Respondent plus those who advised	32
Respondent's adviser only	36
Total	100

likelihood that they would be blamed if things went wrong. A minority of respondents (13, 22 per cent) did not think that their practice could result in allocation of blame. The majority felt that either they themselves (six, 10 per cent), or they plus the colleagues they consulted (19, 32 per cent) or their supervisor/manager (22, 36 per cent) would be blamed if things went wrong (see Table 4.4).

The majority of respondents felt that someone would be blamed if things went wrong. They (26, 44 per cent) saw their employing agency as the main source of blame, though a minority felt that they could be blamed by their clients (six, 10 per cent). Only two respondents mentioned their professional body as a source of blame. These were not vague fears; most respondents had personal experience of things going wrong. Nearly half the respondents (26, 43 per cent) indicated that that they had been involved in a situation or decision that had resulted in a near-miss or an actual incident. Over half the respondents (34, 56 per cent) could cite cases of disciplinary action and in the majority of the cases (24, 70 per cent) the action had resulted in serious consequences: a warning or dismissal for the staff involved.

Despite the possibility of blame, most respondents maintained that this consideration had not influenced their decisions, nor would they have changed their decisions if they knew that they would be protected from blame. Either there was little room for manoeuvre in the kind of situation in which they found themselves or respondents felt uncomfortable at the idea that they might have behaved defensively. There is some indication that the latter might have been the case, as respondents presented themselves as operating with an altruistic and professional orientation to risk management which left little room for defensive, self-interested decision making. For example, respondents were invited to identify the main subject in each situation, i.e. those whom they anticipated would experience the main consequences of their action. As can be seen in Table 4.5, most respondents saw the service users as the prime subject in the situation and did not see the agency as particularly vulnerable or as benefiting. Front-line workers (88 per cent) cited the service user either alone or in combination with other parties as a subject of concern in the overwhelming majority of decisions. Managers also cited the service user but the majority was not as clear cut (67 per cent).

Table 4.5: Subject of concern in risky situations

Subject	Managers (%)	Workers (%)	All (%)
Client	66	88	76
Employee	36	36	36
Agency	35	10	23
Base (=100%)	57	50	107

Note: more than one answer possible; columns do not sum to 100%

In so far as employees were seen as vulnerable or as potential beneficiaries, it tended to be in association with gains or losses for their clients: nearly half the decisions (35, 43 per cent) that involved the client's interest were also seen as involving the employee's own interests. Respondents mentioned themselves as being the sole subject of concern in only 25 decisions (23 per cent).

There was a clear difference in the priorities of managers and workers. Only the managers made any significant mention of the agency as being vulnerable (20, 35 per cent). Only a small minority of workers cited the agency as having an interest in decisions (5, 10 per cent). Respondents did not see the agency as vulnerable to loss through media comment or litigation, but where there was concern about the agency it was more likely to be expressed by managers than workers.

Fifteen (25 per cent) respondents said they took action because they had insufficient information and could not predict potential consequences. The remaining respondents were fairly confident that they knew the likely consequences. On this evidence, uncertainty did not appear to be a major factor in decision making.

Respondents were invited to identify two situations which had been threatening or rewarding. In all respondents identified 105 cases, 70 threatening. The respondents conceived of gains and losses primarily in terms of gains and losses for their clients. Thus, when asked to specify the consequence that was most influential for them in each situation they gave top priority to client rather than agency or personal interests. For example, in 80 per cent of threatening situations interviewees gave top priority to client interests. Managers and workers differed, however. Only 55 per cent of managers who identified a threatening situation put the client's interests as top priority; workers exclusively put client welfare first in these situations.

Although respondents were aware of the potential consequences of non-compliance with agency policies, respondents cited examples in which they chose to disregard the policy. One example of non-compliance concerned a social worker working with a family in which the daughter had alternating violent and depressed episodes. The social worker put together an expensive care package designed to relieve pressure on the family, knowing that resources were not available and that funding could only be found by 'borrowing' from other budgets. This was an infringement of policy and met with disapproval from senior managers. Such outright non-compliance was rare; it was more usual for the situation to be seen as complex, with considerable judgement needing to be exercised about whether and how a particular policy applied.

The most common reasons given for not following policy were either that it was unrealistic (17, 19 per cent) or that it was not applicable (37, 42 per cent). In many cases the agency's policy existed at a high level of generality and needed to be interpreted to fit a particular case. Two front-line workers justified their actions in the following way:

> You have an idea of the policies, but you just have to adapt them to fit the situation.

> [Policies] exist in vague, general terms . . . they give broad guidance.

When interpreting policy, or acting in the absence of policies, respondents drew on their own professional judgement, or on ethical or clinical guidelines issued by a professional body, or on advice from their colleagues or other professionals. In handling a potentially violent confrontation with a mentally disordered man, for example, one respondent relied not on agency policy but on professional advice: 'The psychiatrists have identified certain triggers in behaviour. I knew how to avoid the triggers.'

Managing risk: participation
The strong professional orientation towards service user interests and the use of service user interests to justify decision making and risk management was also evident in respondents' views about participation in the decision-making process. When asked who should participate in high consequence decisions, only a small minority of 60 respondents (7 per cent) felt that such participation should be restricted to experts. The majority felt that it should either include experts plus service users (44 per cent) or should be made by service users alone (18 per cent). It is important to note, however, that when asked about participation in specific decisions, the results were very different. In 65 per cent of the 108 situations, respondents stated that they consulted others about their decisions. Generally, they consulted their colleagues (51 per cent) and only exceptionally did they consult service users or carers (5 per cent). Thus these respondents tended to see decision making in rather paternalistic terms. They justified their decisions in terms of their service users' interest, but they tended to decide what that interest was; they did not consult their clients.

Managing risk: environment
Since the interviews focused on actual situations and decisions it was difficult to examine the extent to which individual practitioners sought to anticipate or respond to risks and the influence of the agency on this preference. However, we were able to explore respondents' perception of threats from the environment and their views of the ways in which the environment impinged on the development of risk policies. We asked them whether they were confident that either their agency or their post would exist in two years' time.

At the time of the interviews, the social services departments and the NHS were undergoing major reorganizations locally as a result of boundary changes and the changes associated with the implementation of the NHS and Community Care Act, 1990, so there was likely to be a high degree of uncertainty. When asked whether they thought their agency would still exist in two years' time, in seven agencies all the respondents were confident that the agency would survive and in the remaining eight agencies only a minority expressed concerns about the survival of the agency. A number of respondents in eight out of the 15 agencies expressed doubts, but they were a minority. When we examined the relationship between employees' perception of their agency's survival prospects and their awareness of agency policy there was no apparent correlation: thus, respondents who were pessimistic about organizational survival seemed no more concerned about risk policies than other respondents.

We also explored interviewees' perception of job security by asking them whether they were confident that their own post would exist in two years' time. While they had been fairly sanguine about organizational survival, they were much more worried about their own prospects. There was a moderately high level of insecurity, with 19 (38 per cent) respondents indicating that their own post might be lost. Managers were marginally more insecure (11, 39 per cent) than workers (eight, 36 per cent). Although this level of insecurity may not seem particularly high overall, it was concentrated in the statutory sector. Of 36 interviewees who worked in the statutory sector, 16 (44 per cent) were not confident that their job would continue, compared to three (21 per cent) of the 14 interviewees in the non-statutory sector. The main reason given for insecurity was reorganization (13), rather than competition (two) or lack of finances (one). As it happened, these fears turned out to be justified for some staff, as reorganization did lead to job losses within the social services department.

In Chapter 3, we provided some confirmation of the prediction-generated cultural theory (Douglas 1992), that organizations performing the same function and operating in the same environment will vary in the ways in which they manage risk. Douglas suggested that this variation could be a response to organizational insecurity. The evidence here is mixed. In a turbulent environment, with a considerable threat to job security, there was little evidence that employees responded to risk in an obviously defensive way. However, this may be because the threat to employment posed by reorganization could not be averted by anything the staff did. It was not a competitive situation: their posts had not become suddenly more dependent on their performance than hitherto.

Although organizational insecurity did not seem to affect the response to risk within individual agencies there was an indication that the environment had impinged on the development of agency risk policies. Respondents were asked why plans, policies, procedures or guidelines which had relevance for risk had been written and the main choices offered were:

- external pressure, i.e. a formal or legal requirement;
- agency learning, i.e. a response to an incident;
- agency anticipation, i.e. an attempt to prevent a possible incident.

Table 4.6: Reasons given for development of agency policies

Reason given	Number
External pressure, learning and anticipation	16
External pressure	12
Agency learning	9
Anticipation	4
External pressure and agency learning	3
Agency learning and agency anticipation	3
External pressure and agency anticipation	1
Other	1

As Table 4.6 shows, the single factor cited most frequently was external pressure. Respondents could give more than one reason, however, and when the total number of citations is considered, external pressure (32 mentions) received only marginally more citations than agency learning (31). Nevertheless, it is clear that, at the very least, respondents believed that pressure to introduce risk policies had come as much from external sources as from within their agency. Manthorpe and Bradley's (1997) discussion of the thinking behind the development of a risk policy within a social services department is consistent with this analysis.

Comment
Respondents did not call on formal agency policies in dealing with risky situations in approximately half of all situations cited. This was largely because agency policies were seen as irrelevant, or because the situation was complex and could only be resolved by professional judgement. Although most agencies were believed to operate with a blameist model, and there was a high risk of blame in the examples given, respondents maintained that they had not behaved defensively, and that the risk of blame had not influenced their decision. Rather, they presented themselves as behaving altruistically and professionally. This orientation towards user interests was also evident in respondents' views about participation in decision making. The majority felt that users should be included in the decision making process, although in practice they appeared to behave paternalistically, rarely consulting users or carers. Where environmental influences were concerned, there was little evidence that organizational or employee insecurity affected risk management, although some of the pressure to adopt specific risk policies was seen as coming from the agency's environment.

CONCLUSION

Our analysis of welfare agencies in Chapter 3 indicated that they were often defensive. The respondents to both our interviews and questionnaires tended to see their agencies as having bureaucratic structures and as being relatively defensive in their responses to risk: the agencies were concerned with account-ability and blame; they reacted rather than anticipated risks; and they re-stricted decision making hierarchically, to a narrow circle of managers or experts. Even where agencies claimed to have adopted a less bureaucratic, more flexible and 'organic' management style they were reported to behave defensively in practice. There was, therefore, a marked gap between the formal and informal accounts of the same agencies. The formal position of the agency was not reflected in the actual ways respondents described themselves dealing with situations and making decisions.

The relative defensiveness of agencies as evidenced in their policy docu-ments was not reflected in the interviews. In the interviews, respondents described themselves operating with an altruistic, user-oriented, professional model of risk management. They indicated that they were aware of agency policy but regarded it as just one source of guidance, to be utilized along with other aids to decision making such as local, national and professional guide-lines. Rather than policy existing in order to limit employees' discretion, the emphasis was on employees exercising professional judgement and actively selecting whatever course of action would enable them to achieve their prime objectives. These objectives were defined primarily in terms of enhancing the interests of the users as the respondents defined them, not as enhancing the respondents' own careers or protecting their agency.

In terms of the literature on welfare organizations this represents a major shift from the findings on the relationship between the formal and informal aspects of agencies. Goffman's and Belknap's studies described a situation in which the formal rhetoric of agencies was therapeutically oriented, i.e. pro-user and in favour of reasonable risk taking, but this was not reflected in the informal processes and relations. The informal structures provided for maxi-mum staff control with minimum effort and therefore excluded reasonable risk taking. The situation reported in our research is different. Agencies ap-peared to have become more conscious of risk issues and therefore there was evidence of policies designed to protect the agency from the adverse con-sequences of risk taking. Many agency procedures were designed to provide bureaucratic control over decision making in conditions of uncertainty. Yet respondents indicated that even where well-developed formal policies existed they needed considerable interpretation, and they still had to exercise judge-ment about how and when to use them. Respondents tended to utilize risk policies when they enabled them to achieve their objectives which they defined as benefiting their clients and disregard them if they felt they were an impediment.

Part of the explanation for the changing relationship between formal and informal structures may be the professionalization of many welfare agencies. Both Belknap and Goffman worked in an environment in which the dom-inance of unqualified but highly experienced staff was being challenged by the increased employment of qualified professional staff such as registered nurses. Although these new professionalized staff were beginning to penetrate the institution, they were still marginalized and the core of the power was maintained by unqualified workers with their firm network of personal relations and their strong cultural traditions. Indeed, Belknap did suggest that one way of reforming the institution was to enhance the power and status of the new professional groups. The situation reported in this chapter is the product of that process. A process of professionalization has taken place alongside the increased bureaucratization of the health and welfare sector.

Since professional staff now play a major role in delivering care and managing welfare agencies, we need to understand their contribution to the management of risk. To understand this further we need to explore in more detail how decisions are made in practice and the ways in which practitioners manage such decisions, and it is to this issue we turn in Chapter 5.

PART 3

PROFESSIONALS, PRACTICE AND RISK

5

PROFESSIONALS, ACCOUNTABILITY AND RISK

Andy Alaszewski, Helen Alaszewski and Larry Harrison

In Chapter 1 we argued that the assessment and management of risk has become a central task for health and welfare professionals. Although modern technologies may have have made living 'safer' for individuals, especially in advanced industrial societies, and enabled individuals to live longer and healthier lives, failures of these technologies can have major and catastrophic consequences. Given the growing complexity and specialization of these technologies, individual citizens and their representatives must rely on and trust experts in the area of health and welfare. In this chapter we examine the literature on the relationship between professionals and the organizational contexts in which they practice. In Chapter 6 we develop this analysis using data from an exploratory study of three groups: social workers, learning disability nurses and district or community nurses.

FRONT-LINE WORKERS AND DECISION MAKING: BUREAUCRATIC CONTROL AND PROFESSIONAL AUTONOMY

In his pioneering work on bureaucracy, Weber (1964) saw the processes of bureaucratization and professionalization as part of the increasing rationality of industrialized society. The bureaucrat was merely guided by more specific rules than the professional. In translating Weber in the 1960s, however, Talcott Parsons took the view that Weber had neglected the analysis of the professions. Parsons polarized professional and bureaucratic authority as possessing two opposing sources of legitimation. Professional authority rested on the public's respect for technical competence, while administrative authority derived from the 'legal competence of office' (Parsons 1964). Parsons believed that the increasing tendency for professional work to be carried out within large organizations had repercussions on organizational structures, as professionals saw themselves as a 'company of equals', and developed their own structures within organizations as an alternative to the established administrative hierarchies.

For Parsons, bureaucratization was the movement towards a form of organization characterized by formal communications, detailed regulations and hierarchical supervision, while professionalization was a movement towards greater autonomy and self-direction, with the minimum of hierarchical differentiation. Parsons' views were developed by Etzioni (1964), who created a typology of organizations based on their relationship to the production of knowledge. Organizations that had professional goals, such as the production of knowledge, tended to be dominated by professional authority. Excessive bureaucratization would be dysfunctional in such organizations, leading to goal displacement. Organizations which had non-professional goals, such as the commercial exploitation of knowledge, tended to be dominated by administrative authority. Professionalization of the workforce could be problematic for such bureaucratic organizations, as it could lead to the pursuit of professional goals, such as high quality, at the expense of organizational goals, such as maximizing profits.

In the context of the present study, bureaucratization and professionalization can be seen as two approaches to the management of risk. In a bureaucracy, risk is minimized through hierarchical control of employees' actions and by limiting employees' discretion in decision making. In the professions, risk is managed through the accreditation of the practitioner's expertise and specialized knowledge, and by maximizing clinical autonomy, to enable professional judgement to be deployed. Whereas Weber saw both processes as complementary mechanisms of social control, in Parsons' and in Etzioni's view the professionals' need for autonomy, for freedom to innovate and take risks, was diametrically opposed to the administrative need for accountability, and the reduction of risk through limiting employees' discretion in decision making.

A number of US studies in the 1960s and 1970s seemed to substantiate Parsons' view of a tension between the two forms of authority. The increasing trend to employing professionals within bureaucratic organizations was leading to conflict, it was claimed, because professionals identified with a professional reference group rather than the employing organization. For example, Scott (1966), studying US welfare organizations, found that professional social workers and lay administrators had two different conceptions of welfare. Social workers were user-oriented and critical of the lack of welfare provision, while administrators wanted to ensure that welfare was provided in a way that served the interests of 'decent, self-respecting, self-reliant citizens'. Others found that bureaucratization impeded the performance of professional tasks (see, for example, Green 1966).

In recent years, the professions have come under increasing criticism for serving their own sectional interests and misusing their monopoly power, and there have been moves to restrict professional autonomy in many countries. In Britain, for example, greater lay managerial control over medical practice followed the Griffiths report and the NHS reforms. Some have seen this as a trend towards the deprofessionalization, deskilling and 'proletarianization' of medicine and other professions (see, e.g., Armstrong *et al.* 1993).

In England and Wales, an apparent process of proletarianization can be seen in the history of social work. Social work in England and Wales developed largely within local authorities after the Second World War, with their emphasis on accountability to elected officers through bureaucratic procedures, hierarchical supervision and the observance of agreed policies. A state-sponsored drive to professionalize social work, evident in the 1968 Seebohm report, was accompanied by a parallel drive towards the greater bureaucratization of local authorities, seen in the introduction of rational planning procedures and corporate management in the late 1960s. This process of bureaucratization accelerated within local authority social services during the 1980s, following the publication of a number of official inquiries into the deaths of children killed by their parents or caretakers, in which social workers and welfare agencies were alleged to have failed to prevent harm.

Howe (1992) argued that the ways in which British public inquiries and government departments conceptualized the problem of child abuse led to policy solutions which were essentially legalistic and bureaucratic. In order to avoid blame, it was necessary for social work agencies to create administrative systems that would identify 'high risk' cases, and facilitate the investigation of suspected families. This translation of the problem of child abuse into a set of judicial and bureaucratic procedures turned social workers into 'passive agents', and contributed to the further bureaucratization of child care practice (Howe 1992).

Thus, social workers could be seen as an occupational group that failed to thrive within a bureaucratic organization, in the sense that their first faltering steps towards professional status appear to have been reversed in a tide of bureaucratization. Yet this is undoubtedly an over-simplification. There is evidence to suggest that there is no essential conflict between bureaucratization and professionalization, and that proletarianization is more apparent than real. In the 1960s, for example, Clark (1966) argued that professional and administrative authority were integrated into a loose federal structure in the US university system; far from being in conflict, the two forms of authority were interdependent. More recently, Weiss and Fitzpatrick (1997) found that general medical practitioners in England did not find the role of Family Health Services Authority (FHSA) advisers in relation to prescribing to be a particular threat to clinical autonomy, and others have noted that bureaucracy either has no effect or actually enhances the autonomy of physicians (Prechel and Gupman 1995).

Anleu's (1992) case study of social workers employed in three welfare agencies also showed little conflict between the autonomy of professionals and the demands of the administrative hierarchy. Indeed, in some ways the bureaucratic regulations within these agencies operated to protect social workers from boundary conflicts and competition with the members of other professions. As in other fields, regulation can benefit the regulated by restricting competition and market entry (Harrison et al. 1990).

Brewer (1996) also argued that conflict was absent because the dynamics of traditional bureaucracies were changing, as more self-employed professionals, such as doctors and lawyers, accepted employee status. These professionals were adopting a new type of group orientation, in which organizational and professional loyalties coincided. Such shifts in allegiance could come about as a result of the dependence which many professionals now have upon complex organizations for essential resources (Anleu 1992). This may lead to a situation of resource dependence, in which reliance on the organization for the provision of scarce resources decreases professional autonomy and creates a condition of interdependence between the professional and the employing organization.

Comment

In the data which we presented in Chapter 4, there was little evidence of a conflict between administrative and professional authority. Some agencies had developed specific policies on dealing with risk, but these operated alongside a reliance on, or an acceptance of, employees exercising professional judgements as to which, if any, policies should apply. Front-line workers were more likely than managers to adopt a professional and user-oriented perspective, and would disregard policy on occasions when it did not facilitate such an approach. Most risk policies appear to have been formulated as broad guides to action, however, rather than as regulations intended to limit discretion. This fits with Weber's original view of the processes of bureaucratization and professionalization as complementary mechanisms of social control, operating at different levels of generality, and it reinforces Clark's (1966) finding that professional and administrative authority could be integrated within a loose administrative structure.

However, in Chapter 4, we treated front-line workers as an undifferentiated group and we did not explore the impact of different patterns of accountability, especially variations in bureaucratic and professional controls on decision making. In the remainder of this chapter we will explore the different patterns of accountability of health and welfare professions before examining whether, in Chapter 6, these have any impact on decision making.

ACCOUNTABILITY

Professionals derive much of their social standing from their specialized expertise. Parsons (1951) argued that their special privileges derived from public confidence in their expertise and in their ability to apply this expertise for the collective good. They had the technical expertise and independence to allocate and utilize public resources efficiently. Parsons explained the suitability of the professions for allocating resources in terms of their 'collectivity-orientation' and contrasted it with the self-interest of the businessman operating in the market in the following way:

the physician is a technically competent person whose competence and specific judgements and measures cannot be competently judged by the layman . . . it would be particularly difficult to implement the pattern of the business world [for the delivery of medical care], where each party to the situation is expected to be oriented to the rational pursuit of his own self-interests, and where there is an approach to the idea of 'caveat emptor'. In a broad sense it is surely clear that society would not tolerate the privileges which have been vested in the medical profession on such terms.

(Parsons 1951: 463)

Parsons was writing during and contributed to the golden era of professional self-regulation. He focused on the key professions, especially the medical and legal professions which at the time enjoyed unquestioned support and tended to operate as independent self-employed practitioners. The social changes of the 1960s and the economic crises of the 1970s undermined this standing and the professions have been subject to increased regulation. The changing relations between the government and the professions in the 1980s in Britain can be summarized in the following way:

The government is seeking to alter its relationship with . . . established professional groups in a number of ways, through:
- the establishment or improvement of market mechanisms and the increase of financial control;
- the reduction in restrictive practices to 'create a level playing field';
- increases in the power and status of consumers, especially by increasing the flow of information to potential consumers;
- inspection of the quality of services.

(Alaszewski 1995: 59)

Part of the pressure to increase regulation comes from growing realization that self-regulation has not resulted in high and uniform standards of professional practice. Indeed, forms of regulation are explicitly designed to create more uniformity in clinical decision making and the development of clinical guidelines in medicine illustrate this move. As Eddy pointed out, there is a high level of variation between the different ways in which physicians make clinical decisions. He noted that much of the variation is created by uncertainty:

Uncertainty creeps into medical practice through every pore. Whether a physician is defining a disease, making a diagnosis, selecting a procedure, observing outcomes, assessing probabilities, assigning preferences, or putting it all together, he is walking on very slippery terrain. It is difficult for nonphysicians, and for many physicians, to appreciate how complex these tasks are, how poorly we understand them, and how easy it is for honest people to come to different conclusions.

(Eddy 1998: 45)

Standing back from a narrow technical perspective, sociologists have accepted that the management of uncertainty and risk is one of the central functions of professions and a major justification of the privileges accorded to them:

The element of uncertainty and the mastery of it have been core characteristics in the social organization of medicine as a profession. Talcott Parsons recognized this feature of medicine when he suggested that 'magic beliefs and practices tend to cluster about situations where there is an important uncertainty factor and where there are strong emotional interests in the success of the action' (1951: 469). Historically viewed, professions became the agents managing the tensions and emotions involved in social situations characterized by uncertainty as this task was transferred from the domestic sphere to the market.

(Riska and Wegar 1995: 201–2)

Today the traditional professions have been joined by other groups such as social workers, who claim that their competence in the management of risk places them alongside traditional professions. As Parton pointed out the management of risk is a core function of professions and social work plays an important role in managing such risks as child abuse.

Professional judgement and decision-making is essentially concerned with the identification and assessment of 'high risk' . . . More than ever it seems that the quality of agency policy and professional practice will be judged in terms of the way they prioritise, assess, plan and respond to risk.

(Parton 1996: 101 and 103)

Although all professions have to deal with uncertainty in their decision making, there is variation in the type of uncertainty which they have to manage and their forms of accountability. We shall deal with the issue of consequences first and then consider the nature of accountability.

HARM, VULNERABILITY AND DANGEROUSNESS

Given the emphasis within the common sense definition of risk of negative consequences, professional accountability is primarily concerned with responsibility for losses. In the commercial sector these losses can be financial losses, hence accountants are responsible to a company's shareholders and others for taking due care to prevent avoidable financial losses. The human services, especially publicly funded services, are primarily concerned with preventing harm to individuals, users, agency employees and the public. This general responsibility to protect is legally known as a 'duty to care' and Lord Atkin in 1932 defined it in a legal judgment in the House of Lords as follows:

You must take reasonable care to avoid acts of omissions which you can reasonably foresee would be likely to injure your neighbour. Who, then, in the law is my neighbour? The answer seems to be persons who are so closely and directly affected by my act that I ought to have them in contemplation as being so affected when I am directing my mind to the acts or omissions which are called in question.

(Lord Atkin in Donoghue v Stephenson (House of Lords) (1932) cited in UKCC 1996: 10)

The clientele of professional practitioners vary in their vulnerability and dangerousness, i.e. in the likelihood that they may be harmed or cause harm to others. Although individual professionals will be dealing with a mixture of users, one way of analysing the characteristics of their case loads is in terms of the likelihood that users will seek their services and can be expected to cooperate with the professionals. Professionals are likely to find it more difficult to predict the behaviours of clients who avoid contact and cooperation and, since the clients themselves are unlikely to be seen as a trustworthy source of information, professionals working with such clients will need to find additional information.

The problems of uncooperative 'clients' and shortage of information on their activities is particularly acute in the police and as Dunningham and Norris pointed out is exacerbated by a 'blameist' organizational culture. They argued that the sociological literature on the police has emphasized:

> the role of uncertainty (Manning 1977), secrecy and solidarity (e.g. Westley 1970) and the defensive nature of the occupational culture in providing strategies for the 'avoidance of trouble', not only from an ambivalent citizenry, but also from punitive and rule bound organization (see, e.g., Chatterton 1975; Norris 1989).
>
> (Dunningham and Norris 1995: 2)

Police officers', particularly detectives', need for information about criminal activities has resulted in the development of strategies for obtaining information, especially the use of informers. As Dunningham and Norris observed, the use of informers generates its own risks which detectives learn to manage using a range of informal strategies:

> Risk is an inherent feature of the detective–informer relationship. For informers to be useful they have to provide intelligence that is pertinent, accurate, reliable and capable of being acted upon. Officers, therefore, have to make difficult judgments as to the status of the information they receive. Fifty-seven percent of officers stated they had been 'let down by an informer' and nearly all handlers spoke of how they could 'never really trust an informer'. In these circumstances the problem becomes how does one trust the untrustworthy and officers have to become adept at managing the risks associated with such uncertainty. Two thirds (68%) of officers stated that they had received information leading to an arrest before registration – suggesting a widespread tendency to limit organisational involvement and oversight until they had established the informer's reliability. While reliability is a major practical issue, more important is whether an informer, in his or her dealings with their handler, is morally trustworthy. It does not matter that their motives are self-serving, what concerns officers is that they are not potentially damaging to their reputations and their careers.
>
> (Dunningham and Norris 1995: 10–11)

Health and welfare professionals such as doctors and nurses usually start from the assumption that users initiate the contact and therefore want the service. It is assumed that users will cooperate and thus the user–professional relationship is based on a voluntary agreement between the professional and the user. In his classic functionalist analysis of the doctor–patient relationship, Parsons argued that voluntarism and cooperation were defining characteristics of the 'sick role':

Finally, the fourth closely related element is . . . the patient has to seek *technically competent* help, namely, in the most usual case, that of a physician and to *co-operate* with him in the process of trying to get well.

(Parsons 1951: 437, our italics)

This assumption underlies much of the analysis of professional risk management in health and social care. Professionals manage risk on the user's behalf because he or she is temporarily unable to manage such risk and the user is expected to cooperate, for:

In order to experience maximum fulfilment in life and reach one's potential it is necessary to take risks. The benefits for the individual can include increased self-awareness, increased emotional and physical independence, a greater ability to make choices, increased confidence and the capacity for further personal growth. These benefits are also compatible with the aims of rehabilitation programmes that focus on maximising to the greatest extent individuals' abilities to regain and retain control over their lives within the limits imposed by their physical and mental capacity. In the field of rehabilitation for older people, practitioners are required to make decisions about the level of risk to incorporate in a care plan for an individual patient.

(Cook 1996: 5–6)

However, the assumption of user cooperation is not always sustainable. As McKinlay identifies in his study of the provision of antenatal care in one Scottish town, even within the health and welfare area some users do not cooperate and may develop avoidance and information withholding strategies as:

Most respondents in the Aberdeen study who underutilized services spent a considerable period of time in and around public assistance agencies, consequently developing techniques to present themselves in a particular way and to withhold information. During observational field work in a maternity clinic it seemed that these tactics were inappropriately transferred to this organisation, calling forth certain unfavourable definitions and responses from the clinic staff.

(McKinlay 1975: 371)

It is important to note that vulnerable individuals may also wish to avoid the attention of professionals in order to sustain an identity as normal and maintain their independence (Edgerton 1967).

Comment
A key role of human service professionals is to manage personal risks, especially the risks generated by the behaviours of service users. An important element in managing such risk is the anticipated level of service user cooperation, and in particular their willingness to provide reliable information. If the professional can treat the user as a trustworthy and reliable source of information, then the assessment and management of risk is simplified. However, if it is anticipated that the user is likely to be uncooperative and will withhold

information then assessing and managing risk becomes more difficult. Strategies need to be developed for obtaining reliable information and, as in the case of the use of informers by the police, these strategies may generate their own risks.

EMPLOYMENT, THE LAW AND ETHICS

The second dimension of risk management relates to ways in which professionals' decisions are scrutinized and the external controls and checks over their actions and decisions. In the previous section we discussed one influence on professional practice, that is the nature of their relationships with clients. Traditionally professions have enjoyed high levels of autonomy in decision making but as Light (1995: 35) pointed out: 'The end of professional dominance involves the state and other major players entering the governance structure of the profession to monitor its work and restrain its economic and clinical activities.'

The erosion of professional autonomy has come from a number of potentially conflicting sources or in Light's terminology, countervailing power. These include:

- the agencies which employ professionals;
- the state, especially through the law;
- the bodies which licence professional practice.

Accountability to employers

There is a difference between professionals who are self-employed and therefore sell or contract to provide clients with services and professionals who are employed by agencies and therefore provide services to clients on behalf of agencies.

Self-employed professionals, such as many lawyers and general medical practitioners, are personally accountable for their actions and can therefore be personally held to account for them. Although medical specialists in both the UK and USA tend to be hospital employees, in some ways they are treated as if they were self-employed. For example, they must have their own medical insurance and can be personally sued when their patients experience harm as a result of their negligence. In the USA the growth of litigation has had a major impact on medical practice both in terms of the high cost of medical insurance and the reluctance of individual practitioners to practice in areas where there is a high risk of litigation:

In 1991 it was reliably estimated that the annual premiums and self-insurance cost of medical professional liability in the United States was approximately $9 billion. By the 1980s the spiralling cost of malpractice insurance had already caused many physicians either to leave the profession or to abandon certain high risk practices such as obstetrics. This had a devastating effect on rural practitioners. As an example, the state of North Carolina in the 1980s passed legislation known as the Rural

Obstetrics Care Incentive Program to underwrite the malpractice premiums of rural obstetricians. Between 1988 and 1992 the cost of that programme tripled.

(Jones 1996: 18)

Thus accountability within the medical and legal professions tends to be to clients via the courts or to professional colleagues rather than to the employing authority. Bosk argues that surgeons take on the responsibility for disciplining their own colleagues by excluding non-professional involvement in the process:

The uncertainty which the surgeon routinely faces in making a diagnosis and pinpointing a precise causative agent for therapeutic misadventure accounts for a great deal when explaining why surgeons discipline errant colleagues as they do and when explaining why normative rather than technical breaches are the more serious errors . . . My claim is that postgraduate training of surgeons is above all an ethical training. Subordinates are harshly disciplined when they violate the ethical standards of the discipline. They are promoted and accepted into the ranks on the basis of their ethical fitness.

(Bosk 1988: 540–1)

Other professions, usually those that are accorded limited professional status, such as social workers, derive their primary identity and authority from their status as employees of specific agencies. They are expected to work within the framework of agency policy and practices and, if serious harm occurs to a client, then as long as they can demonstrate they were implementing agency policy, it is the agency that is held responsible. The emphasis on agency and managerial control of front-line worker practice can be seen clearly in the following description by a member of Her Majesty's Inspectorate of Probation of the probation manager's responsibilities for supervising the work of front-line staff:

In practice this means that first-line managers should know 'inside out' each case involving a potentially dangerous person held by staff members accountable to them. They should be involved in key decisions relating to the management and supervision of such cases and have the professional skills, knowledge and expertise to advise staff, endorse or guide the direction supervision takes and coach them to enhance their professional skills. They should have the professional confidence to liaise and negotiate with other professionals, and with senior managers in their own agency, to ensure that resources are available to provide high quality supervision, that staff receive adequate training and supervision and that the agency's framework of policy and practice guidance is sufficient.

(Lawrie 1997: 303)

The difference between the professional autonomy of medical practitioners and the accountability of social workers to their agencies is clearly stated in the following legal judgment:

The fundamental fallacy is to regard a local authority social worker as being in the same position as a General Practitioner under the National Health Service. One is not more professional than the other. It is just that they are different. It is no part of the duties of the National Health Service to treat patients. Its function is to provide Doctors who will do so. The resulting relationships are (a) employer and employed Doctor and (b) Doctor and patient. By contrast, it is the duty of a local authority to care for children and to play a part in the process of their adoption. For this purpose local authorities employ social workers. The resulting relationships are (a) local authority and employed social workers and (b) local authorities, social workers and the 'client/patient' of both.

(Donaldson 1982: 363 cited in Guy 1994: 263–4)

The law and accountability

Although the government can influence professional practice indirectly through its influence on employers, especially in the public sector, a more direct mechanism of influence is through direct regulation, especially through the law. All professional practice takes place within a legal framework and professionals may be sued in the civil courts if their negligence results in harm or loss. However, for a professional to be sued it must be established that the professional had a duty of care to the client and that the client experienced a loss as the result of the actions or inactions of the professional.

However, the law may influence professional practice in a more direct way. In some professions the law provides an enabling framework; it provides a 'licence' to practice with associate privileges and immunities. In other areas, the law imposes specific responsibilities and therefore controls.

The state regulation of the medical profession gives a clear example of a regulatory framework designed to provide a licence to practice. Since the formation of the NHS in 1948, successive governments have stressed that competent medical practitioners have 'clinical autonomy', i.e., a licence to practice. The government places the responsibility on the profession to regulate itself to ensure that all practitioners are competent. For example, the 1995 Medical (Professional Performance) Act provides the General Medical Council with powers to investigate allegations of deficient professional performance but, as the Department of Health press release announcing the Act makes clear, it is a system of self-regulation;

The Act provides protection by ensuring that:
- doctors whose performance is alleged to be seriously deficient are professionally assessed;
- when appropriate, doctors take remedial action if they wish to remain in practice; and
- where required for the protection of the public, conditions on the doctor's registration and practice can be imposed, including suspension from the GMC's register to prevent the doctor from continuing to practice.

(Department of Health 1997a: 1)

This use of the law as a mechanism for enabling and self-regulation contrasts strongly with the situation in which the law is used to impose specific responsibilities. For example, probation officers' accountability to their agencies is reinforced by specific legislation:

Agencies such as the probation service have long had a responsibility to try to prevent all further offending by everyone under supervision. This duty was emphasised by the 1991 Criminal Justice Act which enshrined in law probation services' duty to protect the public from offenders subject to community sentences.

(Lawrie 1997: 301)

It is possible to argue that for some professions, there has been a process of 'juridification' whereby professional action is not only subject to, but has actually become part of, the legal system. King (1995) argued that a series of high profile child abuse inquiries in the 1970s and 1980s exposed social work's inability to manage the uncertainties associated with child protection. In particular, social workers have been unable to effectively identify and prevent abuse with any certainty. As a result, in England, the child abuse problem has been redefined as a legal rather than as a social work problem in the 1989 Children Act. King's view was that the Act redefines the task of social work. Rather than being responsible for guaranteeing children a safe and healthy environment in which they can thrive, social workers have become responsible for investigating cases of child abuse and producing evidence which enables the courts to reach a sound decision. The emphasis shifts from the child and his or her family's welfare, which the social worker judges, to identifying and protecting the rights of children and families, which the social worker may need to challenge. King identified a similar process of juridification in Scotland, especially after the 'Orkney Inquiry' (Lord Clyde 1992). King argued that the Children's Hearings in Scotland were designed to provide informal and lay mediation between social work agencies and families in an attempt to provide an agreed solution to a child's problem. With the growth in recognition of child abuse, there is an increasing emphasis on rights and on legal representation. Thus the hearing is less of a lay mediation and is increasingly a quasi-legal arbitration.

Professional ethics

Professions providing human services vary in their degree and pattern of self-regulation. At one extreme are professions such as teaching which in Britain are effectively regulated by central government civil servants and at the other extreme are professions whose training and practice are regulated by statutory bodies which are dominated by the profession.

The current position in social work represents an intermediate position. As Guy pointed out, the role of a professional council might be to regulate both training and practice:

The core component of a General Social Work Council is the facility to judge the competence of an aspiring social worker who wishes to join the

register, and judge the competence of those already registered to continue
to practice.

(Guy 1994: 261)

The Central Council for Education and Training in Social Work has been
responsible only for the regulation of professional training not for regulating
practice. As Parker (1990: 15) pointed out, this is currently the responsibility of
the employing authorities. The case for a council which regulates both training and practice is based on the scale of risk implicit in social workers'
decisions and the consequent need for additional scrutiny of their decisions
and actions:

> Stripped of all embellishments the case for a General Council has rested
> upon the conviction that since social workers are entrusted with the
> exercise of considerable discretion they should be subjected to mandatory
> regulation over and above the control exercised by their employers. Such
> regulation, it is argued, provides an important measure of protection to
> those people whose lives are affected by what social workers do. In social
> work good judgements, compassion and integrity are at a premium, not
> least because many of those with whom social workers become involved
> are vulnerable and dependent in states of crisis or despair.

(Parker 1990: 15)

Since British social workers do not have a social work council, they do not
work within the framework of an enforceable code of professional practice and
therefore make their decisions within the framework of the policies and
practices of their employing authority and/or specific legislative requirements.

The development of a general social care council, to which the current
government is committed, will place social workers in a similar position to
nurses. Although nurses employed by agencies such as hospital or community
trusts must make decisions within the framework of agency policy and
practices, they also have to make decisions within the framework of the
'Code of Professional Conduct' of their professional licensing council, the
United Kingdom Central Council for Nurses.

The UKCC's code of conduct established a clear framework of professional
accountability:

> As a registered practitioner, you hold a position of responsibility and other
> people rely on you. You are professionally accountable to the UKCC, as
> well as having a contractual accountability to your employer and account-
> ability to the law for your actions . . . You have both a legal and a
> professional duty to care for patients and clients. In law, the courts could
> find a registered practitioner negligent if a person suffers harm because he
> or she failed to care for them properly. Professionally, the UKCC's Pro-
> fessional Conduct Committee could find a registered practitioner guilty of
> misconduct and remove them from the register if he or she failed to care
> properly for a patient or client, *even though* they suffered no harm.

(UKCC 1996: 8 and 10, our italics)

The UKCC does acknowledge that there may be a tension between agency policy and professional requirements and makes it clear that registered practitioners have a duty to report their concerns if resources are inadequate or if for other reasons they feel unable to provide a safe level of care:

> As a registered nurse, midwife and health visitor, you are personally accountable for your practice and, in the exercise of your professional accountability, must . . .
>
> 11   report to an appropriate person or authority, having regard to the physical, psychological and social effects on patients and clients, any circumstances in the environment of care which could jeopardise standards of practice;
>
> 12   report to an appropriate person or authority any circumstances in which safe and appropriate care for patients and clients cannot be provided;
>
> 13   report to an appropriate person or authority where it appears that the health or safety of colleagues is at risk, as such circumstances may compromise standards of practice and care.
>
> (UKCC 1996: 21)

Within the UKCC code of professional conduct, however, there are unresolved tensions. The code indicates that nurses and other registered practitioners should both encourage patient autonomy (and by implication risk taking) but at the same time protect patients and others from the consequences of risk taking and minimize the risks to which patients and others are exposed. As Cook pointed out this creates dilemmas for practitioners seeking to provide care and manage the associated risks and she explored the nature of these dilemmas within rehabilitation care. This work:

> demands and requires some risk taking, against a background of increasing litigation for negligence and injury. Nurses have been particularly exercised by these dilemmas. An examination of their situation indicates that professional codes of practice are not always helpful, sometimes stipulating levels of knowledge and practice that are difficult to achieve and sometimes providing what appear to be contradictory directives. The danger of this situation is that nurses and other practitioners may avoid risk taking altogether. The consequences of this for patients may, however, be damaging, in that independence may be decreased and maximum potential may not be achieved.
>
> (Cook 1996: 12)

CONCLUSION

Effective assessment and management of risk is at the centre of professional practice in human service professions. As we argued in Chapter 2, central government policies create dilemmas because they are based on contradictory objectives and the resolutions of these tensions and the associated dilemmas are passed to health and welfare agencies. As discussed in the first section of this chapter, welfare agencies do have policies and practice, but we could find no evidence of these frameworks being treated as rigid rules and regulations. Rather professionals retain discretion and choose when and in which context to implement agency policy. This effectively means that agencies have delegated the responsibility for managing the dilemmas of workers and they have accepted this responsibility.

Thus the nature of professional practice is strongly influenced by the perceived uncertainty and difficulty of decision making and the ways in which professional decisions and actions are scrutinized. Uncertainty is increased when professionals cannot rely on service users for reliable and accurate information.

The intrinsic uncertainties generated in providing care can be exacerbated by the mechanisms used to review professional decisions. Medical practitioners enjoy a high degree of autonomy from employers, a degree of legal privilege and their decisions are subject to professional peer review. Social workers have very limited formal discretion and their decisions are subject to scrutiny especially by their employers. Nurses can be seen as intermediate, they are professionally accountable for their actions but are subject to the scrutiny of employers.

One of the key issues this raises is whether different patterns of scrutiny influence the ways in which risk is managed and in particular whether scrutiny by professional colleagues is different from scrutiny by managers. This differentiation relates to the classic debate over professionalization and bureaucracy. In his pioneering work on bureaucracy, Weber (1964) saw the processes of bureaucratization and professionalization as part of the increasing rationality of industrialized society. The bureaucrat was merely guided by more specific rules than the professional. In translating Weber in the 1960s, however, Parsons took the view that Weber had neglected the analysis of the professions. In Chapter 6, we will explore the ways in which different patterns of accountability influence professional decision making by comparing the ways in which social workers, learning disability nurses and district nurses perceive risk and make decisions related to vulnerable service users.

6

PROFESSIONALS AND PRACTICE: DECISION MAKING AND RISK

Helen Alaszewski and Andy Alaszewski

In this chapter we will develop our analysis of professionals and decision making using evidence from a study which examined the ways in which professionals perceived and managed risk. In the first section, we describe the study. In the second, we examine the significance which the participants in our study attached to risk and how they defined it. In the third section, we will examine in detail how the respondents managed risk in their everyday decision making.

THE STUDY

The data in this chapter is derived from an exploratory study of social workers, learning disability nurses and district nurses. These three groups were selected because they performed similar functions but were subject to different forms of accountability. All the participants in our study were providing care and support for vulnerable people in the community. They visited clients in their own homes where they assessed client's needs and/or provided services. Although they could draw on the advice and expertise of other practitioners and mobilize resources such as residential placements or hospital admission, when they visited a client they were often on their own and had to make immediate decisions using the information available at the time.

The participants

Although the three groups operate within a similar environment and provide similar services, they have different patterns of accountability. As we argued in Chapter 5, social workers operate within the framework of their employing authority, but the Central Council for Education and Training in Social Work (CCETSW) only regulates training not practice. Although social workers involved in child protection operate within a well-developed legal system, social workers in our study were providing care for adults generally and only came into contact with the courts or other parts of the legal system if the mental incapacity of their client created a specific problem. Thus there was an emphasis on organizational or bureaucratic patterns of accountability. Both learning disability nurses and district nurses worked within the framework of their contract of employment but this influence was balanced by the requirements of the UKCC's Code of Professional Conduct. They also worked within teams, community learning disability teams or primary health care teams. The teams tended to reinforce the 'professional' aspect of accountability albeit it in different ways. In learning disability services, teams tended to be well-established with well-developed multi-disciplinary decision-making mechanisms, for example case conferences. This emphasized the professional standing and contribution of learning disability nurses. In contrast primary health care teams were poorly developed and district nurses were 'paraprofessionals' working within the context of decisions made by general medical practitioners (Øvretveit 1993).

Individual practitioners' decisions are likely to be influenced by their level of experience, the more experienced practitioner is likely to be more confident and therefore may perceive and react to risk in different ways to the less experienced practitioners. We looked at the perceptions of students, newly qualified practitioners and experienced practitioners. We restricted our analysis of decisions to those made by practitioners, since we considered students would be under direct supervision. Since the study was exploratory we decided to select a small group of individuals and work intensively with them. To reduce the possibility of atypical findings we decided to select at least two individuals in each category, i.e. two student social workers. Thus we included 28 individuals in our overall sample, though in this chapter we only use data from three of the groups (17 individuals) (see Table 6.1).

Initial interviews

The study explored respondents' perceptions and management of risk through interviews and practice diaries. All practitioners had an initial briefing interview designed to explore their overall perception of risk. The interviews were semi-structured and perceptions were explored using leading questions. The first question was designed to explore respondents' definition of risk. Respon-

Table 6.1: Sample for exploratory study

	Social workers	Learning disability nurses	District nurses
Students	2	2	2
Inexperienced practitioners	2	2	2
Experienced practitioners	2	1	2

dents were asked 'What do you understand by risk?' This was followed by a question exploring respondents' view of the significance of risk for professional practice, 'How important do you think risk assessment and management is in professional practice?' This was amplified by a third question which focused explicitly on the significance of risk for decision making; 'How do you think risk influences decision making?'

The fourth question in this sequence explored respondents' perceptions of the ways in which risk underpinned practice: 'Which aspects of practice would you associate with risk?' Although the emphasis was on exploring respondents' own views, prompts were also used to explore possible underlying views. For example, when the respondents had had an opportunity to provide their own definition of risk, the interviewer explored their support for elements of risk identified in the literature. For example the interviewer would ask 'Is uncertainty something you'd associate with risk?' to check whether the respondents saw risk in probabilistic terms. In this chapter we draw on the replies to the leading questions unless we clearly specify that the data came from the prompt questions.

Diaries

While the interviews explored respondents' perceptions of risk and its impact on practice, we also wanted to capture 'real' clinical decisions and then to explore with participants the risk implications of these decisions and how they were managed. One way of 'capturing' decisions is to actually observe them. However, observation is both labour intensive and intrusive. Observing 10 shifts per participant would take 280 days or nearly a year of researcher time. Furthermore, since some of the participants in this stage of the research were trainees at an early and formative stage of their career, it was possible that direct observation would have a considerable impact on them. We decided to use a less intrusive approach to capturing decision making. We asked participants to act as observers and to record their observations in diaries. We were following the approach developed by Zimmerman and Wieder:

> Individuals are commissioned by the investigator to maintain . . . a record over some specified period of time according to a set of instructions . . . The technique we described emphasizes the role of diaries as an observational log maintained by subjects which can then be used as a basis for intensive interviewing.
>
> (Zimmerman and Wieder 1977: 481)

Zimmerman and Wieder's study was similar to ours as they were also concerned with hypothesis generating:

> the diarist's statement is used as a way of generating questions for the subsequent diary interview. The diary interview converts the diary – a source of data in its own right – into a question-generating and, hence, data-generating device.
>
> (Zimmerman and Wieder 1977: 489)

Following an initial interview each participant was given a diary. The diary was designed to capture some of the decisions and situations in which the participant was involved in clinical practice so that the risk and learning implications could be explored in a debriefing interview. Thus diarists were invited to record for each shift the general activities that took place, two or three decisions and to comment on whether they felt they had been adequately educationally prepared to make the decision.

The number of entries depended on the nature and length of the placement. Generally, the research team aimed to have at least 10 complete entries though in some cases it was only possible to obtain five entries. However, this still ensured that each diarist identified at least 10 decisions.

When the participants had completed their diaries, the researcher undertook a preliminary analysis of the diary identifying and classifying decisions. Once this had been completed the researcher selected two contrasting decisions. These then formed the debriefing interview. The researcher explored with respondents how and why the decision had been made, their involvement in the decision, the risk implications of the decision, the extent to which they had been prepared for the decision and the teaching and learning implications of the decision.

PRACTITIONERS' PERCEPTION OF RISK

In this section we shall discuss respondents' perception of risk. We start by considering the ways in which practitioners define risk. We then examine practitioners' perceptions of the importance of risk in their practice. Finally, we examine how their views on the ways in which risk influences practice in general decision making is specific.

Defining risk

For most of the respondents risk was a taken-for-granted word. When invited to define risk, most respondents had to stop to think about the answer. In some cases respondents, even after thinking about their answer, still did not define risk but used the term as if the meaning could be deduced from the usage:

Interviewer   What do you understand by risk?
Nurse   By that you mean me personally how I would see it, risk to myself or to my clients or both?
Interviewer   Both.
Nurse   I think through each day you face different risks and certainly as regards to the clients I work with, a lot of it I think comes from your knowledge and experience . . .

However, following a pause for reflection, most respondents were able to say what they understood by risk. One type of definition was an 'every day' or 'common sense' definition in which risk is defined in terms of negative consequences of an action or as a danger or hazard which (without intervention) would result in a negative consequence. This type of definition can be seen in the following extract from an interview with a social work student:

Interviewer What do you understand by risk?

Student I think risk is anything that puts a person or themselves or other people in danger [anything] from leaving a cigarette burning in an ashtray to living with a violent partner.

A similar definition was provided by an experienced district nurse:

Interviewer What do you understand by risk?

District nurse If I look at the work point of view. I look at risk as looking at areas that could be a problem to me and how I could prevent myself getting into a situation or causing damage to one of my clients or to myself, and from a work point of view, risk itself in general is you have a go at it don't you and see what the outcome is.

Although the overwhelming emphasis in the interviews was on risk as the negative consequences of actions or situations (see Table 6.2), it was possible to identify other subsidiary themes. Some of these themes could fit alongside the negative consequences theme, for example the issue of probability or chance, whereas others were more difficult to reconcile, for example risk as empowerment.

The view of risk as probability could in some cases be seen as an elaboration of risk as negative consequences as shown by the following extract from interview with a social work student:

Interviewer What do you understand by risk?

Student Risk erm, the chance of something undesired happening . . . working out the probability of it actually happening.

A similar set of ideas was evident in the extract from the following interview with a district nurse student:

Interviewer What do you understand by risk?

Student An actual or potential situation may occur which has adverse effects on patients.

In some interviews, respondents developed their ideas a stage further. Although accepting risk could involve negative outcome and probability, they were also aware of the positive outcomes which a risk taker might be trying to achieve. They therefore argued that risk involved choice and a balancing or weighing up of negative and positive outcomes or consequences. This approach is clear in the following extract (learning disability nursing student):

Interviewer What do you understand by risk?

Student I think as a task or an objective . . . a person wishes to do that's attached with that are possible and probable outcomes ranging from good outcomes to bad outcomes which a person has to weigh up. The individual has to weigh up as to whether the possibility of achieving this task . . . I don't see risk just as physical violence or suicides or anything, it ranges from making a cup of coffee to suicide or even just sitting on a chair.

Some respondents developed this argument further and implied that risk-taking could be seen as a positive experience for clients and indeed that it was a right that clients should have. The practitioner had to balance the client's rights to take risks against the professional's obligation to ensure safety and to minimize harm. The respondent in the following starts with a risk as danger definition but qualifies it by drawing attention to client's right to make choices (experienced social work practitioner):

Interviewer   What do you understand by risk?
Social worker   That's a big question, er, I think risk is a level of potential danger.
Interviewer   Do you want to say anything else about it?
Social Worker   Um, it can go from one extreme to the other and I think each individual's perceptions of risk can vary quite dramatically as well, or the element of risk, erm from a social work point of view, I guess it would be around erm danger versus individual rights to make those choices I guess.

As Table 6.2 indicates, the main emphasis was on risk as danger, though it was also possible to recognize awareness of risk as probability and risk as potentially empowering. Although the number of respondents was very small there were some differences between the three occupational groups. Given the strong emphasis on organizational accountability in social work practice, we anticipated that social workers would place greatest emphasis on the negative consequences for risk to avoid blame if things went wrong. This was indeed the case but there was some evidence that risk as client choice was also important.

We were aware that risk is a complex concept and that most of our respondents had received little formal training in risk. We therefore used prompts to explore respondents' awareness of the different facets of risk. We explored the consequence aspect of risk with prompts about safety, vulnerability and abuse; the probability aspect with prompts about uncertainty; and risk-taking aspects with prompts about choice.

The prompt confirmed that consequences (and preventing negative consequences) was seen as an important aspect of risk. In particular, safety was

Table 6.2: Definitions of risk

	Consequences	Uncertainty	Choice
Social workers	8 (100%)	1 (12.5%)	2 (25%)
District nurses	5 (100%)	1 (20%)	
Learning disability nurses	2 (50%)	2 (50%)	1 (25%)
All	15 (88%)	4 (24%)	3 (18%)

more closely linked to risk than vulnerability and abuse. This can be seen in the following interview with an experienced social worker whose main role was to assess the needs of adult clients in the community. Her response to the prompt was an amplification of her initial definition:

Interviewer   What about safety, is that an aspect of risk?

Social worker   That is crucial I mean if you are talking about risk I mean some people don't realize they are at risk I mean like leaving a gas on, I mean people with a memory impairment will say they don't leave the gas on even though we have evidence that they do leave the gas on, the gas cannot only be a detriment to their lives, life threatening for them, it also could be for the neighbours and for other members of the family.

When prompted, respondents also showed awareness of the probabilistic elements of risk as in the following interview (inexperienced district nurse):

Interviewer   Is uncertainty something you would associate with risk?

District nurse   Yes I think sometimes there is that uncertainty because there is the element of needing to do something to help the person but there's also the element of that person being responsible for themselves . . . the risk is minimized I feel by trying to introduce things that may prevent the risk of occurring so it's sometimes like a balancing act, you're thinking 'right what's in place now? What could we do to lessen the possibility of that risk happening?'

When prompted most respondents also recognized that risk often involved situations in which there was choice, indeed the uncertainty about outcomes meant that there were actually choices to be made and in particular an opportunity to provide users with choice. For example, a student social worker responded to the prompt about choice in the following way:

Interviewer   What about choice, is that something you'd associate with risk?

Student   Ch-, yeah because choice is obviously something which you're trying to leave in the hands of the service user but I mean sometimes risk assessment may come, may come with dilemmas of whether you take away choice or allow choice, give, or give choice, so that's quite disempowering.

However, some practitioners felt that although providing choice might be desirable in many situations there were other factors, usually concerns with safety which meant that there was in practice no choice:

Interviewer   What about choice, is that something you would associate with risk?

District nurse   Not always.

Interviewer   Why do you say that?

District nurse   You've still got the pressures all around you. I would maybe see a risk and refuse to do that but the environment and the job might say well that's your job you do it, I'll give you an instance from that

Table 6.3: Responses to prompts

	Consequences	Uncertainty	Choice
		Number of respondents	
Social workers	6	6	5
District nurses	4	5	4
Learning disability nurses	4	3	4
All	14	14	13

point of view, with your shortage of staff and you know you are working under par that's a risk, that's a risk to yourself and to the patient but who does the work, so sometimes I haven't got a choice but to just get my head down.

Indeed, some respondents felt that choice was more part of rhetoric than reality:

Interviewer   What about choice, is that something you would associate with risk?

District nurse   The word is used loosely, even cynically. I am a believer in empowerment and I try to give patients choice but 99 per cent of the time there is no real choice.

Although respondents' 'gut reaction' was that risk could be equated with negative consequences, as Table 6.3 indicates when prompted nearly all respondents agreed that there were other dimensions to risk.

Comment

Our interviews with practitioners indicate that all of them felt that risk was a very important part of practice. But it was also clear that risk was treated as a taken-for-granted concept. Their 'gut reaction' was to see it as something nasty and unpleasant, as the negative consequences of failing to identify and deal with dangers and hazards. However, when prompted, it was clear that they had an awareness of the complexity and multi-facetedness of risk. Some respondents did not need any prompting to show their awareness of complexity of risk. The following extract is taken from an interview with a social work lecturer. This lecturer was not a 'diarist' but was interviewed as part of a related study of risk in social work education.

Interviewer   What do you understand by risk?

Lecturer   Well one thing I must say is that people seem to use it in different ways and have different emphasis and have different ways of using the terms that are quite legitimate not so much through lack of understanding . . .

I would distinguish between, it was off the top of my head . . . risk analysis/assessment they're virtually . . . and risk management and may be risk taking those three things . . .

My understanding of [risk] is quite tight but not something everyone would agree with that the risk is the likelihood of something untoward happening, I use the word untoward but you could use the word dangerous and nasty images, you know something undesirable happening may be better, that is risk so to assess the risk in a situation is to make a decision about the likelihood of a particular undesirable thing happening so whether it is a child being harmed, by an adult committing suicide or an older person going home from hospital and falling and various things like that.

Risk management . . . I would make a distinction between risk management and that is how an agency or a worker manages risky situations it might involve that agency tries to minimize risk or minimize the comeback problem of people taking risks and I see that as being quite a defensive approach.

Now risk taking is another important thing that is to do with the rights to take risks and people's quality of life they give balance between risk minimization and risk taking so for instance if someone is in hospital and are due to go home and the medical staff are recommending that they go to a residential home the social worker might take the view that the person has got a right to take risk, you know life without risk is not very good – and understanding what risk is in life in general so we might talk about enabling people to take risks.

The importance of risk

All respondents felt that risk was an important part of practice. Indeed, most respondents thought that risk virtually permeated professional practice as illustrated by the following comment from an interview with a student nurse: 'It's the cornerstone – it underpins everything.' A learning disability student nurse felt that risk assessment and management was fundamental to professional practice:

Interviewer How important do you think risk assessment and management is in professional practice?
Student They go hand in hand with one another, you've got to be able to manage your resources, you've got all the resources and manpower to manage as well therefore you've got to be aware of what risks are apparent in that situation you're managing to enable you to say I can give in order to deploy your resources adequately . . .
Interviewer When you say hand in hand did you mean that you think it comes into everything you do?
Student More or less yes, I think it sort of runs parallel to one another whatever a decision a manager has to take . . . the possible, probable outcomes are there so you've got to weigh up the the benefits and disadvantages of not doing it so I think they run concurrently all the way through.

Some respondents felt that risk was becoming increasingly important in the context of increased pressure on resources. The following extract taken from an interview with an experienced social work practitioner illustrates this:

Interviewer Well do you consider it an important part of your practice?
Social worker I guess more and more so with social services we're more and more limited as to what we can actually provide erm and it tends to be a lot, a lot of intervention rather than prevention work . . .

Risk and professional decision making

Respondents saw risk as a key element of clinical decision making and most respondents felt it underpinned their decisions. The following extract provides concrete examples:

Interviewer How do you think risk influences decision making?
Social worker It's got to be it's a central part of it because I mean we can't leave somebody at home if they are at risk from themselves but we've got to assess what that risk is, how will we get to alleviate that risk, is it possible to alleviate that risk and leave them in the surroundings where they wish to be, if it is not possible we try to ascertain the risk and discuss it with the client and the carers. A real example of that was I had somebody who refused point blank to go in to hospital although this lady was terminally ill . . . It took a lot of coaxing and I had her family on the door chuck the key in to reception and said she's your responsibility we're not doing any more with her . . . she was at risk we couldn't leave her at home . . .

Often risk was an issue because the practitioner had to resolve a dilemma:

Interviewer How do you think risk influences decision making?
District nurse Very much so if we go back to lifting and handling, you see a need you haven't got the resources but risk factor is that if you do something and you do some injury whether it's to the patient or to yourself the repercussions are more severe than actually not doing things.

Some respondents felt that risk was becoming an increasingly important element of professional decision making and saw this as a product of increased litigation and increased awareness among patients of their rights. A learning disability nursing student considered:

Interviewer How do you think risk influences decision making?
Student I think it influences it a lot more than it did, a lot more people are aware of risk than they were four or five years ago and I think personally speaking the reason for that is basically down to litigations with the Community Care Act and the Patient's Charter and everything I think people are more scared of courts . . .

Thus it is clear that the respondents saw risk assessment as central to professional practice and in particular felt that it was closely linked to professional decision making. In the next section we will explore specific aspects of practice which respondents associated with risk.

Risk and practice

When invited to comment on the relationship between risk and practice, the majority of respondents felt that risk permeated and affected all aspects of professional practice as can be seen in the following extracts; the first from an interview with an inexperienced district nurse and the second from an interview with an inexperienced social worker:

Interviewer   What aspects of practice would you associate with risk?
District nurse   The main well there's all sorts of risk, mental health care programme you're looking at preventative measures, isolation, depression, loneliness, ultimately suicide . . .

Interviewer   Which aspects of practice would you associate with risk?
Social worker   All aspects of my practice are associated . . . I have care managers that I supervise and we go through clients, the work they've undertaken with clients and also clients' needs during supervision because there may be risk there, there's risks that they may feel I'm not an appropriate practice teacher and I may feel that they are not doing their work and that may be putting the client, or themselves or the department at risk.

In this area there was some difference between social workers and nurses that could be related to the stronger influence of organizations over the practice of social workers. When social workers discussed practice they tended to emphasize resource issues:

Interviewer   Which aspects of practice would you associate with risk?
Social worker   One of the main elements is identifying need but not having the resources. How much would it cost to bring in private services?

In contrast nurses tended to emphasize aspects of clinical practice and direct relationship with providing services to users:

Interviewer   Which aspects of practice would you associate with risk?
District nurse   Working one-to-one [with a user] so it's there the majority of the time.

Although most respondents were able to discuss the relationship between risk and practice, their response to the leading question was generally relatively bland and uninformative. As with the definition of risk it is clear that they felt that risk was an important part of their practice but did not seem to have seriously thought about how risk influenced their practice prior to the interview. Indeed, in many cases, the answers to the leading questions on the importance of risk and aspects of practice were virtually interchangeable –

most respondents felt that risk was very important as it was integral to their practice. They did not necessarily link it to any specific aspect of their practice. We therefore used prompts to examine two alternative approaches: hazard management and user empowerment. To examine the hazard management dimension we invited respondents to comment on safety and protection issues. To explore the empowerment issue we invited respondents to comment on clients and risk decisions. Most respondents agreed that they were both hazard managers and user enablers. One experienced social worker defined her role as being primarily a bureaucratic resource manager implementing routine decisions, so was neither empowering nor hazard managing:

Interviewer   What about empowering clients to make choices?
Social worker   The official line is that you let clients make choices. The unofficial line or the reality is that you give them the information, tell them about the funding, the Residential Care Panel system. Really it's disempowering, you're dictating to them telling them what there is but there is very little choice.

Hazard management, in terms of maintaining a safe environment or in terms of protection, was seen as a key part of professional practice:

Interviewer   Which aspects of practice would you associate with risk?
District Nurse   I'm not sure what you mean by that.
Interviewer   Is maintaining a safe environment an aspect of practice you would associate with risk?
District nurse   Yes . . . I mean it could be a risk of someone falling with the room being cluttered or it could be the other types of risk we've already discussed like gas fires, etc.

Managing hazards was seen as a key element of professional practice. Indeed, providing a safe environment and protection was seen as the first priority. Once the practitioner had made sure that there were no hazards then he or she could devote attention to other activities:

Interviewer   Is safety something you'd associate with risk?
Student social worker   With my limited knowledge of risk assessment that is my priority basically, if the client's safe then OK my practice may be somewhat oppressive until I develop whatever but I mean as long as they're safe that's the priority.

Most practitioners saw user empowerment as an important objective but one which might be difficult to achieve. A newly qualified learning disability nurse, having defined risk in terms of negative consequences, when asked about the enabling aspect gave the following example:

Interviewer   Is enabling the client to make decisions an aspect of practice which you associate with risk?
Nurse   Enabling? Yes. I took a girl out swimming and there were a whole variety of behavioural problems – choice of cubicles, the locks on the doors. I let her get changed by herself, giving her independence but being there. If a person has a bad experience it could stop them

wanting to gain experience. If you are walking past a car and the lady becomes violent, then you wouldn't take her down a narrow street. You have to be aware of the dangers.

In the following extract, a social work student identifies empowerment as an aspiration which may only be achieved in certain circumstances.

Interviewer   What about enabling the client to make decisions? Is that an aspect of practice you'd associate with risk? I know you have talked a little bit about choice haven't you?

Student   Yeah, cos, but I mean, obviously if you're trying to empower your clients and let them be independent and make choices for themselves there is, there comes a point where you have to make them aware of the consequences of their choices and sometimes if the client is particularly vulnerable you may have to take away their choice.

Practitioners were aware of the tension between client protection and empowerment and some respondents identified a third role, using their professional judgement to balance the tension:

Interviewer   Is choice something you would associate with risk?

District nurse   Oh yes very much so. There has to be that choice . . . I could go in and say do this this and this and [clients] might sit there and nod their head and think well I'm going to have to do it and then the risk would still happen because it's not what the person wants so it's like negotiating and setting a contract quite often with that person.

Comment

Respondents saw risk as an essential part of contemporary professional practice and in particular they felt that most clinical decision making involved risk. However, it was also evident that practitioners treated risk as taken-for-granted. They defined risk primarily in negative terms as hazard, danger and negative outcomes of action. However, when practitioners' understanding of risk was explored through prompts, it was clear that the dominant definition was a 'gut reaction' which masked an awareness of risk as uncertainty and risk as choice. Practitioners' definitions of risk were linked to their perceptions of the influence of risk on their professional practice. They emphasized their role as the managers of hazards but through prompts, it was possible to identify other roles, for example, enablers or empowerers who could facilitate risk-taking by clients. Some respondents were also aware of a tension between these two roles and identified a third possible role of the practitioner as a mediator, balancing protection against user empowerment.

In the next section we will develop the analysis of professionals and risk by examining the actual decisions which professionals make and how they identify and manage these decisions.

> **Example 6.1: Newly qualified learning disability nurse's decision**
>
> *Context:* Taking a young woman to a swimming pool and to observe her
> from a 'distance'.
> *Decision:* (i)   To take young woman to the pool and 'give her space'.
>   (ii) To take her out of the pool when she started to become
>   agitated.
>   (iii) To buy her a drink so she could calm down.

RISK AND DECISION MAKING IN PROFESSIONAL PRACTICE

Newly qualified practitioners, decision making and risk

In this section we examine the decisions made by newly qualified practitioners
and to provide a depth of analysis we concentrate on one student from each
category of practitioner.

Newly qualified learning disability nurse
Example 6.1 is typical of the one-to-one therapeutic intervention made by
learning disability nurses. The main issues within the process concern the
client's welfare and well-being.

In the debriefing interview, the nurse described her decision in terms of
potential benefits and costs for the client:

Interviewer You're taking her swimming and then on that particular day
    you decided to give her a little more space – why had you decided to
    do that?
Nurse Well we had been concentrating a lot on her behaviour . . . so I'm
    trying to balance giving her a little more independence, giving her the
    opportunity to sort of control her own behaviours . . . There is a
    slight risk element, say we're at the machine and she wants a choco-
    late bar it would be much easier to do it all for her really because when
    she's doing it herself she gets it wrong and she'd get very angry that
    she'd made the wrong choice, lash out at somebody else or myself.

Newly qualified district nurse
The decisions identified by newly qualified district nurses were client focused
but often involved conflict between different stakeholders in the client's care.
In Example 6.2 this conflict was so great that the nurse felt she had to suspend
a pre-discharge meeting as there were family disagreements.

The diarist, in her initial description of the situation, recognized the
complexity and the range of different issues involved:

Interviewer It was where you had to advocate for the client . . . I wonder if
    you could tell me a little bit about the meeting . . .?

Example 6.2: Newly qualified district nurse's decision

Context: Meeting held at a residential unit with client and his family to discuss when and where he should be discharged.
Decision: (i) To hold meeting with client and family.
(ii) To act as an advocate on behalf of client against some of his family.
(iii) To suspend the meeting to protect the client.

District nurse   Right . . . this man had initially moved to this area . . . following his wife's death and a number of other issues regarding the family . . . there seemed to be a lot of friction within the family about what should happen to him and then what the client wanted as well . . . Really I suppose I felt as if the person from the ward should have been dealing with that [family tension] and it was like everyone was sat letting it happen and I thought hang on a minute it shouldn't be going on like this it's not getting us anywhere and the Consultant flitted in and went out, the daughter was very concerned about her father's future need but she also had concern about the financial side of it. Her brother just wanted money from her father . . . also the brother had recently come out of hospital . . . with his own mental health problems so there was a lot of issues apart from what was going on with the client.

Newly qualified social worker's decision
As newly qualified practitioners, they were not only involved in more complex situations but also involved in prioritizing the allocation of resources rather than directly providing client care. Example 6.3 involves a series of decisions by a newly qualified social worker who was seeking to provide a package of support for a terminally ill woman who wanted to return home. Her husband and two adult children were willing to support her but her husband was severely disabled and her children had jobs and other family commitments. The social worker felt that the community social work team was inflexible in their approach and decided to seek management support for a more flexible package of support.

Example 6.3: Newly qualified social worker's decision

Context: Assessment of the needs of a terminally ill client due to be discharged from a hospice.
Decision: (i) To carry out a full community care assessment.
(ii) To recommend a flexible package of care and support in the community.
(iii) To seek the support of higher manager for the package.

The social worker identified the central issue as one of resources:

Interviewer What were the potential outcomes positive or negative of taking it higher?

Social worker The potential outcomes were that they would meet the need in a way that was appropriate but that it would be expensive, well cost obviously it was going to be more expensive to purchase the needed support . . . there's no point them answering the questions and me filling in the forms if they don't get the support that's needed.

To achieve the desired outcome, the social worker needed to negotiate a suitable allocation of resources with her service provider colleagues and when they were not willing to provide what she assessed to be an adequate level of service she had to appeal to higher management.

Interviewer What were the anticipated consequences of the decision?

Social worker I just feel that if I've assessed, if I've done an assessment it's a thorough assessment of need and if that need doesn't get addressed be it for difficulties with flexibility, be it because of financial reasons or whatever then what's the point of me doing it in the first place?

Comment
Generally, when newly qualified staff were involved in complex decisions they were using their professional judgements. Learning disability nurses tended to be involved in one-to-one therapy with users, so their decisions tended to be simpler and more client focused. Newly qualified social workers and district nurses tended to address more complex issues. The most complex involved managing the dilemmas created by differing and conflicting interests.

Experienced practitioners, decision making and risk

Although experienced practitioners dealt with a range of routine and relatively straightforward situations and decisions, they also had to make decisions in which there were complex issues and we focus on these more complex decisions in this section.

Learning disability nurse
The example we have taken from the diaries completed by learning disability nurses deals with the nurse–client relationship, but the situation is complicated by the moral issues raised by the practitioner's desired course of action, which is to persuade the client to have a contraceptive implant and the involvement of carers and other professionals (see Example 6.4).

In the interview, the nurse initially discussed the decision in terms of her personal relationship with the client. She justifies her decision not to pursue the discussion with the client in terms of the client's situation, it was not an urgent issue as the client did not have a boyfriend.

Nurse What actually happened was that the lady had referred herself to the Learning Disability Team. One of the issues that came out . . . was about contraception . . . I made contact with the lady and started

Example 6.4: Experienced learning disability nurse's decision

Context: A sexually active young woman living at home and attending a
further education college.
Decision: (i)   Took client to visit GP to discuss contraception.
(ii) Although implant recommended does not pressurize client.
(iii) Defers discussion to later date.

weekly visits so that I could build up a bit of rapport . . . I did discuss
with her this issue I felt . . . We did actually make an appointment
which she agreed to go and have a chat with the GP because she
wasn't actually on the patient list in the past . . . now we went and
had a chat with the GP and talked about an implant . . . we left the
surgery and we had a chat and she seemed quite strong about she
certainly didn't want the implant and wasn't actually sure whether
she wanted anything at all – she didn't have a boyfriend or she said
she didn't have a boyfriend at the time and didn't appear to be
interested in sex.

However, as the interview progressed it became clear that in the nurse's view
the user was probably sexually active and that an important factor in her
decision had been the views of other participants in the decision-making
process, especially the user's social worker:

Nurse [On] subsequent visits it appeared that she was certainly keen on
men and certainly did know a lot more about sex than she let on to
me . . . she has actually gone back to the GP willingly and has now
had contraception prescribed through her choice . . . In hindsight
when I actually look back on it her social worker knew her a lot better
than I did at the time and obviously I felt that she wasn't ready for
contraception at the time or interested in men but I saw that she was
when I got to know her. What would the consequences have been for
her if she had got pregnant in that time.

Although the nurse felt that the outcome of the situation had been
satisfactory and that she had empowered her client by enabling her to make
an informed decision, she did not feel comfortable with the involvement of
other professionals in the process. The nurse clearly felt she had been able to
deal effectively with aspects of the decision-making process, especially her
relationship with the user but there were other aspects of the process that were
less satisfactory which potentially undermined her efforts. In particular, she
was unable to control the activities of other professionals.

Experienced social worker
Social workers were also very much concerned with the welfare of clients but
many of their complex decisions involved working with resource and/or
service constraints. Given the complexity of clients' needs and the rationing

Example 6.5: Experienced social worker's decision

Context: An elderly couple, severely disabled wife, husband is the main carer but has injured back, husband cooks meals.

Decision: (i) A full community care assessment.
  (ii) Recommendation that couple should be provided with person to cook one meal a day.
  (iii) Recommendation not accepted.

of resources, most of the complex decisions involved juggling resources. We have selected an example in which the social worker identified a way of enabling a client to remain in his home and provide care for his wife but was unable to negotiate the necessary package of support from her department and was therefore unable to prevent the negative consequences which she anticipated (see Example 6.5).

At the start of the interview, the diarist described the context of her decision and her proposal for dealing with the situation:

Social worker Oh yes – this was the couple I went to I did an initial assessment . . . the husband who was the main carer and had back injury and was finding it very difficult to care for her [his wife who had Parkinson's Disease] . . . the outcome of the assessment was that I felt they needed somebody to go in and undertake cooking a hot meal for them. Now I knew the chances of me getting that service provision would be very slim because we do have meals on wheels provision and we can have somebody to go in and do a shopping service to buy ready made meals that can be reheated but this couple had never had ready made meals, didn't want to even consider it and wouldn't consider meals on wheels.

The social worker made this recommendation to her senior who held the budget for community care services but he was unable to accept the recommendations as there were in his view alternative services which were both cheaper and more cost effective. The social worker was forced to convey her senior's decision to the client and to try to negotiate an alternative package of care. The alternative was not acceptable for the clients and the negative consequences which the social worker had been trying to avert took place. The husband fell and had to be hospitalized. The social worker felt that she had been trying to act in the clients' best interest but resource constraints and her inability to persuade her senior meant that a preventable accident happened. There was, however, a positive outcome as the accident made the client realize that he had to accept the service offered.

Social worker I think we've had some negative outcomes and some positive, I've had negative outcomes in the way that he did end up falling but we've had positive outcomes in the way that because of that fall we've looked at ways that we can try and enable them both to stay at home by giving them support, aids adaptations and I've also arranged for an OT to go in and do a kitchen assessment to overhaul his kitchen, to make it more appropriate for him to get to his cupboards and make it easier for him.

This social worker saw herself as acting for and on behalf of the client but since resources were explicitly rationed she needed to negotiate with the budget holder to get the necessary resources. Initially, she was unable to match the clients' needs to the available services. Following the accident she was able to do this, the services remained the same but the clients were now willing to use them.

Experienced district nurse
From an early stage in their training district nurses dealt with complex issues. What changed was their level of responsibility. Although experienced nurses worked with general practitioners their advice and guidance had considerable influence over the decision made by GPs. In Example 6.6 we have selected a situation in which the GP had formal and legal responsibility for deciding how much morphine a dying patient should receive and the district nurse provided the information which shaped the decision.

The case concerned a frail elderly woman who was living in a residential home and had deteriorated following a chest infection. The district nurse came under pressure from the manager of the home to increase the amount of morphine being supplied. In her view this was to participate in an assisted death:

District nurse   The manager related it to the family, the family were amazed she was still hanging around when she should have died a couple of weeks back . . . Now I had to put my foot forward in that by saying 'no sorry the syringe driver is there to make her comfortable and that's what it is doing', so there was quite a lot of pressure to try and instigate that but I think we've got to look at the needs of the patient rather than the needs of the people around us. Nothing is ever said directly.

The district nurse conveyed the request to the GP with the information that the current dosage was adequate, in her opinion, for pain relief. The GP accepted her view and as the woman's condition deteriorated so the dose was increased:

Example 6.6: Experienced district nurse's decision

Context: A terminally ill woman with pressure sores and chest infection.
Decision: (i)   To provide patient with a syringe driver for pain control.
          (ii)   Refusal of request from residential home manager to increase dose of morphine.

District nurse   The positive side that I see is that we did keep the patient pain free because obviously within 24 hours it was reviewed and there was a necessity to up the dose so I feel that we did give the patient . . . the problem occurs obviously when we're looking at an age group that people think well you wouldn't do it to a dog and I think we've got to be as practitioners to be seen to be humane in what we are doing. Positive side for me was I felt I was doing the best for the patient, now we're talking about an elderly, frail 100-year-old lady.

Although this situation involved complex ethical issues and a conflict of interest, it was interesting to note that when asked about the training implications of the decision, the nurse saw these in technical terms, improved communication. Improved communication would only make the ethical issues clearer, it would not resolve them.

Comment

As practitioners progress and become more experienced so the situations which they deal with become more complicated in terms of the complexity of client needs, possible tensions within families and possible strain between the various practitioners involved in a user's or family's support. At the same time the support that professionals receive declines. Whereas students have mentors or practice teachers whom they can consult and who take responsibility for their decisions, experienced professionals must rely on their own judgement. Indeed, in some situations they are in conflict with their own employing agency. This was particularly evident in social work where managers often have a dual role as managers and supervisors.

FINAL COMMENT

Respondents saw risk as a central part of professional practice. They defined risk in terms of negative consequences, but when prompted they were able to see risk in broader terms. They related consequences primarily in terms of benefits or harm to users.

Clients and their families formed the central focus of decisions. Practitioners justified their decisions in terms of their consequences for the welfare of their clients. Decisions became difficult when there were conflicts in the process, especially where the practitioners' perceptions of the clients' best interests conflicted with the expressed wishes of one of the participants in the decision-making process. Practitioners tended to deal with these issues as they came up on a relatively pragmatic and common sense basis. There was little evidence that practitioners had been trained in formal decision-making processes and that they used structured decision-making processes. For example, though many of the decisions were made in the context of uncertainty there was little evidence that practitioners attempted to formally assess probability and that such assessments influenced their decisions and actions.

What is conspicuously absent in practitioner accounts of their decisions is agency policy. Although practitioners were clearly aware of agency policies they did not treat them as rigid rules. Employees actively used both agency policies and professional guidelines to achieve their client-oriented goals, rather than reacting to judicial and bureaucratic procedures as passive agents. From a top-down perspective, the response to risk appeared to be determined by agency policy, but from a bottom-up perspective, policy documents were only one source of information to be utilized in reaching a decision.

PART 4

CONCLUSION

7

HEALTH AND WELFARE: MANAGING RISK IN LATE MODERN SOCIETY

Andy Alaszewski

This chapter draws together and develops the main themes of our analysis of risk and its relationship to health and welfare. It begins by examining some of the conceptual structures which underlie current approaches to health and welfare. It then explores the ways in which these systems of thinking have influenced the development of health and welfare services and how an effective understanding and use of risk can help resolve some of the dilemmas within the provision of these services.

THE ENLIGHTENMENT, MODERNITY AND RISK

The modern study of society began in the late seventeenth and eighteenth century and was associated with a European intellectual movement, the Enlightenment. During the 'Age of Reason', radical intellectuals or philosophers applied the scientific method developed in the sixteenth century to society. These intellectuals were interested in improving social conditions and were committed to 'progress'. They felt reason and rationality would form the basis of human progress. In their view progress was impeded by the irrationality of pre-modern systems of thought which would be exposed as superstition by the rationality of science. Systematic scientific investigation would reveal the real facts. The cumulation of knowledge would provide the basis for the effective control and management of both nature and society. Thus science and the rationality on which it is based would provide 'man' with control over and ability to shape 'his' destiny.

Enlightenment thinking

Underlying enlightenment thinking were a set of interrelated assumptions. These included: rationality and reason as a sole basis of truth and knowledge; the ability of science based on rationality to provide comprehensive knowledge about the natural and social worlds; and the ability of 'man' to use scientific knowledge to liberate 'himself' and improve society and generate progress.

Reason and rationality

The first major assumption underpinning Enlightenment thinking related to the ways in which humans understand and interpret the natural and social world in which they live. Enlightenment thinkers identified two contrasting approaches to understanding and knowledge; the traditional and the modern. In the traditional approach, understanding and interpretation was based on the uncritical acceptance of 'received wisdom' such as religious faith or belief. Thus the major sources of knowledge were 'revealed' to man by God, for example the Holy Bible. Individual knowledge was always limited and partial in comparison to the universal knowledge of God, the ultimate authority. Individual thinkers were always struggling to understand and interpret divinely inspired sources and there were divine mysteries that were inexplicable by humans.

In contrast their modern or scientific approach was based on the collection of information from the natural and social worlds and its interpretation using systematic human reasoning. Thus the individual, especially the individual thinker, became both the source and sole arbiter of all knowledge. The French philosopher, Descartes, identified the key role of the individual thinker as the arbiter of truth when in his *Discours sur la méthode*, originally published in 1637, he resolved to:

> Accept nothing as true which I did not clearly recognize to be so: that is to say, to avoid carefully precipitation and prejudice, and to accept nothing in my judgements beyond what presented itself so clearly and distinctly to my mind, that I should have no occasion to doubt it.
>
> (cited in Williams 1990: 32)

The contrast between the traditional and scientific approach can be seen in a variety of debates and Enlightenment thinkers used the successes of the previous generation of natural scientists as proof of the superiority of the rational scientific method, particularly citing the debates on the nature of the universe.

Religious thinkers using Biblical sources argued that the earth was the centre of the universe and the other celestial bodies orbited around the earth. By the sixteenth century, the systematic observation of celestial bodies by astronomers was generating increasing information about the precise movements of the moon and the planets. This information was increasingly difficult to reconcile with the belief that these celestial bodies orbited around the earth. In 1510 a Polish astronomer, Copernicus, advanced an alternative theory. Copernicus reasoned that the earth and planets orbited the sun. In 1543 he published his theory with supporting statistical evidence (*De revolutionibus orbium coelestium*, On the Revolutions of the Celestial Spheres). Copernicus' theory was the basis of further investigation and was popularized by the Italian astronomer, Galileo Galilei, who used the newly invented telescope to make observations which confirmed Copernicus' theory. Galileo's criticism of the astronomy in the Bible brought him into conflict with the Church which sought to suppress his work as it undermined the authority of the Bible and traditional beliefs based on it.

> 'The astronomical language of the Bible', he [Galileo] suggested to the dowager Duchess of Tuscany, was 'designed for the comprehension of the ignorant.' This in 1616, earned him a summons to Rome, and a papal admonition. And Galileo's praise for Copernicus put Copernicus onto the Index (of publications prohibited by the Catholic Church). When Galileo persisted, however, and published his *Dialogo dei due massimi Sistemi del mondo* (Dialogue on the two main world systems, 1632), which expounded the superiority of Copernicus over Ptolomey, he was formally tried by the Inquisition, and forced to recant.
>
> (Davies 1996: 508)

Science and knowledge
The second assumption of Enlightenment thinking related to the extent of potential knowledge. Traditional thought was seen to be based on irrationality and unpredictability. Interventions by gods or spirits meant that the world was essentially unpredictable as events such as miracles or the Second Coming could occur at any time and could not be understood by normal human reasoning. In human affairs, divine intervention was associated with concepts of fate or predestination. Thus a central problem for theologians was how to reconcile apparent contradictions such as free will and individuals' ability to choose their own actions with the absolute power of God and His divine and absolute power to control all human events.

In contrast scientific thinking was based on a systematic approach and the search for laws which would both explain and predict events. In this approach the collection of information through the senses, through observations made by the individual, was important, but the individual could only differentiate real from false knowledge through the rigorous application of reason to observation and in particular a questioning or sceptical approach to all observation and received wisdom. Descartes describes this approach in his *Discours sur la méthode* in 1637:

> because I wanted to devote myself solely to the search for truth, I thought it was necessary . . . that I should reject, just as though it were absolutely false, everything in which I could imagine the slightest doubt, so as to see whether after that anything remained in my belief which was entirely indubitable. So, since our senses deceive us sometimes, I wished to suppose that there was nothing which was as they make us imagine.
>
> (cited in Williams 1990: 35)

The implication of this approach was that if a belief could withstand this rigorous critical process it could be accepted as the truth. Reason was the basis of truth and of the correct understanding of natural and social events. If an observer had sufficient knowledge and understanding, the underlying cause of each and every event could be explained. Thus all events were essentially predictable. Sir Isaac Newton's (1642–1727) experiments and theories seemed to confirm this. His Laws of Motion could both explain and predict the movement of physical objects and his concept of gravity could explain why the earth moved round the sun. Rational thinking had no place in unexplainable and unpredictable events such as miracles. Everything was essentially knowable and predictable.

Whereas pre-Enlightenment scientists had concentrated on the natural world, the Enlightenment focus shifted to include society and its constituent units, individuals and their relationships.

By the nineteenth century the scientific method had been so successful that the French scientist, Laplace, was confident enough to claim that total knowledge was feasible, that scientific laws would enable scientists to explain and predict all natural *and social* events:

> The success of scientific theories, particularly Newton's theory of gravity, led the French scientist the Marquis de Laplace at the beginning of the nineteenth century to argue that the universe was completely deterministic. Laplace suggested that there should be a set of scientific laws that would allow us to predict everything that would happen in the universe, if only we knew the complete state of the universe at one time. For example, if we knew the positions and speeds of the sun and the planets at one time, then we could use Newton's laws to calculate the state of the Solar System at any other time. Determinism seems fairly obvious in this case, but Laplace went further to assume that there were similar laws governing everything else, including human behavior.
>
> (Hawking 1988: 53)

Progress and perfectibility: the uses of knowledge

The development of rationality and science were linked to ideas of human progress. Traditional societies were seen as essentially static and 'timeless'. Knowledge and the technologies based on this knowledge, were both fixed, limited and 'primitive'. Such societies were vulnerable to disasters, famines and epidemics as they lacked the knowledge to predict such events and the technologies to prevent them. The explanations for such disasters tended to be irrational, i.e. divine retribution. The Black Death, an epidemic of bubonic, septicaemic and pneumonic plague, which swept Europe between 1347 and 1350 killing approximately a third of the population was associated with an outbreak of 'irrational behaviour':

> The conviction reigned that God was punishing mankind for its sins . . . Though the Church as an institution was weakened, popular religiosity increased . . . Intense piety came into fashion: people felt that God's wrath must be placated. In Germany, huge companies of flagellants flourished until suppressed on orders from (the Pope in) Avignon. Communal scapegoats were sought. In some places lepers were picked on; elsewhere the Jews were charged with poisoning the water . . . It was the signal for wholesale pogroms.
>
> (Davies 1996: 411–12)

The development of science and rationality meant that knowledge and understanding could accumulate and replace irrational beliefs and behaviours.

In the eighteenth century there was a sustained movement to collect and systematize all available knowledge in collected works or encyclopaedias. The most famous of these collections of knowledge was published in France:

> In France, the great project of the *Encyclopédie* or *Dictionnaire raisonné des arts, des sciences, et des métiers*, undertaken by Denis Diderot (1713–84) and Jean d'Alembert (1717–83) . . . appeared in Paris in 17 volumes of 16,288 pages between 1751 and 1765, with further supplements, illustrations, and indexes appearing up to 1782. It was programmatic, opinionated, anticlerical, and highly critical of the regime; and its editors were regularly harassed by officialdom. Yet it was a monument to the age. It aimed at nothing less than a summary of the whole of human knowledge.
>
> (Davies 1996: 599–601)

The accumulation of knowledge was both an end in itself and also a means to an end. It would provide the basis for replacing superstition with rationality. Although the systematic study and control of nature was an important aspect of science, particular emphasis was placed on understanding society. Thus the Enlightenment is associated with the development of the systematic study of political systems by Hobbes, Locke and Montesquieu and of economic systems by Adam Smith. These thinkers paid particular attention to the constituent unit of society, the individual or citizen. Not only did an effective understanding of political or economic systems need to be based on an understanding of individual behaviour, but an effective understanding of the political and economic system could be used to develop systems which would enhance the well being of *all* citizens.

Jean-Jacques Rousseau used this approach to develop the concept of a social contract (originally published in 1762 as *Du contrat social*). He argued that the majority of individuals in eighteenth century society existed in a state of virtual slavery. Their human rights had been taken away by despotic absolute monarchs. He argued that individuals should be liberated through a radical change creating a new political system based on a social contract. This contract would limit the powers of the state and protect the rights of each citizen. Rousseau's ideas influenced both the authors of the constitution of the United States of America and the French revolutionaries creating their new republic.

There was a reaction in the nineteenth century against rationality and Romantic writers stressed the importance of the irrational or emotional elements of human nature. However, within the social sciences rationality continued to dominate. Auguste Comte developed a new 'science of society' based on a 'Philosophie positive' (1850–4) or positivism. He envisaged a corps of 'social engineers' reconstructing society using the slogan 'To know in order to foresee, to foresee in order to prevent'.

At the same time Karl Marx was developing his theory of capitalism and communism. The Communist manifesto was originally written in 1847–8 by Marx and Engels and included the phrase: 'Let the ruling classes tremble at a Communist revolution. The proletarians have nothing to lose but their chains. They have a world to win' (Marx and Engels 1962: 65). This was a conscious echo of Rousseau's famous statement that 'Man is born free, and everywhere he is in chains.'

Marx argued that nineteenth century society and all previous eras were based on the exploitation of a majority by a minority. He believed that such exploitation could be ended and individuals liberated through the creation of the ideal society brought about by the revolutionary action of the oppressed class, the proletariat. This communist society would mark the climax of human progress (Giddens 1990: 154).

The limits of Enlightenment thinking

Although Enlightenment thinking remains a strong influence on social theorizing in the twentieth century, its main assumptions have been subject to critical comment. Its failure to recognize uncertainty and risk meant that it was seriously flawed.

The limits of rationality

Enlightenment thinking is essentially dualistic; it is based on the contrasts between opposites. The most obvious contrast is between rationality and irrationality and this in turn underpins the contrast between traditional and modern society. In traditional society knowledge and beliefs are based on and justified by superstition whereas in modern society, knowledge is based on rationality and the accumulation of scientific knowledge. Thus the process of 'modernization' is one in which traditional irrational beliefs are replaced by modern rational systems of thought.

This polarization between traditionalism and modernity is misleading. Anthropological studies of traditional societies show that rationality both exists and plays an important role in such societies while similar studies in modern society, indicate the persistence of non-scientific or irrational folk beliefs. For example, Helman, in a widely reproduced study of lay health beliefs makes the following observation:

> What has been the impact of three decades of health education, television programmes about health, and easy access to doctors and hospitals, on traditional beliefs about illness? Whatever happened to folk remedies and old wives' tales? A study which I conducted on medical folklore in a north London suburb suggests that these old beliefs about illness and health *can* survive the impact of scientific medicine and in some cases may even be reinforced by this contact.
>
> (Helman 1984: 10, emphasis in the original)

Evans Pritchard in his classic study of the ways in which a traditional African tribe, the Azande interpreted and responded to misfortune demonstrated that for the Azande rational and magical explanations coexisted and contributed to a total explanation of observed phenomenon. He argued that certain aspects of Azande understanding were based on a rational understanding of natural causes. However, magic thinking was used to explain particular circumstances, especially the uniqueness of an event which explained why it resulted in harm to a specific individual.

In speaking to Azande about witchcraft and in observing their reactions to situations of misfortune it was obvious that they did not attempt to account for the existence of phenomena, or even the action of phenomena, by mystical causation alone. What they explained by witchcraft were the particular conditions in a chain of causation which related an individual to natural happenings in such a way that he sustained injury. The boy who knocked his foot against a stump of wood did not account for the stump by reference to witchcraft, nor did he suggest that whenever anybody knocks his foot against a stump it is necessarily due to witchcraft, nor yet again did he account for the cut by saying that it was caused by witchcraft, for he knew quite well that it was caused by the stump of wood. What he attributed to witchcraft was that on this particular occasion, when exercising his usual care, he struck his foot against a stump of wood, whereas on a hundred other occasions he did not do so, and that on this particular occasion the cut, which he expected to result from the knock, festered whereas he had had dozens of cuts which had not festered. Surely these peculiar conditions demand an explanation.

(Evans-Pritchard 1937: 67–8)

What was missing in Azande thinking was not rationality but the concept of chance or probability. Natural causes plus mystical causes explained everything. There is no room for uncertainty, for 'accidents' or 'coincidence'. The index of *Witchcraft, Oracles and Magic among the Azande* (Evans-Pritchard, 1937) did not include an entry for risk or any risk related concept. Evans-Pritchard described the certainty of the Azande in the following way:

Azande regulate their economic activities according to a transmitted body of knowledge . . . [which] suffices for their everyday tasks and seasonal pursuits. When in spite of it they fail, *the reasons for the failure is known in advance* – it is due to witchcraft.

(Evans-Pritchard 1937: 80, our italics)

Evans-Pritchard noted (pp. 80–3) that the Azande were unable to explain in detail the ways in which witchcraft and other 'mystical' processes worked but they were clear that these explained everything that could not be explained by 'natural' processes.

What characterizes modern society is not the replacement of irrationality by rationality but the reduction of certainty and the development of mechanisms to deal with uncertainty, i.e. the awareness of chance and the development of means of assessing and managing risk. As Giddens notes (1990: 27), 'there doesn't seem in fact to be a notion of risk in any traditional society'. Beck makes the same point in a different way:

Risk society begins where tradition ends, when, in all spheres of life, we can no longer take traditional certainties for granted. The less we can rely on traditional securities, the more risks we have to negotiate. The more risks, the more decisions and choices we have to make.

(Beck 1998: 10)

Within Enlightenment thinking progress is associated with the growth of rationality and by implication a process of secularization. This may have been the case in Europe but in other parts of the world, modernization has been associated with the revitalization of tradition especially religion. Turner describes the link between modernization and religious revival in Islamic societies in the following way:

> The central theme of modernization was, however, legitimized in terms of a return to classical Islam, that is the Islam of ascetic, literary monotheism. Once Islam was liberated from its folk traditions and from foreign accretions, Islam could emerge as a dynamic and progressive component of the reform of society. The return to the Qur'ān was in practice used to bring about profound changes in Islamic life.
>
> (Turner 1994: 87)

The limits of science

In the twentieth century science itself has been subject to critical analysis. The uncertainty it has generated has become a central issue in terms of the use of science and the nature of the knowledge. Scientists working in the seventeenth century were acutely aware of the limits of contemporary knowledge but there was also confidence that given sufficient time and work, it would be possible to know and predict everything and that such knowledge would be beneficial for society. In late modern society not only can science not guarantee certainty but it has itself become a source of uncertainty and threat.

Just as Newtonian physics promised certainty plus social benefits, so the work of Einstein introduced risk into science, both in the uncertainty of its subject matter and uncertainties about the benefits of the products of science. The uncertainty generated by post-Einstein physics is most clearly seen in the sub-atomic world of quantum mechanics:

> In general, quantum mechanics does not predict a single definite result for an observation. Instead, it predicts a number of different possible outcomes and tells us how likely each of these is . . . Quantum mechanics therefore introduces an unavoidable element of unpredictability or randomness into science. Einstein objected to this very strongly, despite the important role he had played in the development of these ideas. Einstein was awarded the Nobel prize for his contribution to quantum theory, nevertheless, Einstein never accepted that the universe was governed by chance; his feelings were summed up in his famous statement 'God does not play dice.'
>
> (Hawking 1988: 55–6, see also, Kane 1998: 78)

As Hawking pointed out total knowledge and therefore complete explanation or prediction is not feasible:

> The uncertainty principle signalled an end to Laplace's dream of a theory of science, a model of the universe that would be completely deterministic: one certainly cannot predict future events exactly if one cannot even measure the present state of the universe precisely!
>
> (Hawking 1988: 55)

The very success of science has created major uncertainty about its social benefits. The development of nuclear physics has created the potential for a nuclear holocaust and global destruction:

> After science's vigorous participation in the atomic nihilism of the Cold War – despite the calls for non-involvement in nuclear weapons research from Albert Einstein and Leo Szilard, among others – its claims to be merely a value-free 'servant of knowledge' rang deafeningly hollow. Science facilitated a risk with our very global existence: on pure level of species survival our mistrust of the Enlightenment's greatest tool is deeply rooted.
>
> (Kane 1998: 78)

The limits of progress
The Enlightenment thinkers dreamed of human progress and the ideal society. The cumulation of knowledge through the use of reason would generate control both of nature and of society, liberating humanity from its dependence on nature and all the disasters associated with this dependence. However, the use of science and associated technologies has not prevented disasters, it changed the scale and frequencies of some disasters and created new ones. Disasters in pre-modern societies may have been more frequent but they also tended to be smaller in scale than in modern society. Modern disasters can be on a global scale.

The globalization of disasters can be seen in environmental changes such as the erosion of the ozone layer and global warming. Both these changes are a product of technological development and have been associated with increased level of harm. The manufacture and release of CFCs has been linked to the erosion of the ozone layer:

> A good example of the limits of the predictive power of science is the way in which CFCs were hailed as wonder chemicals when first produced in bulk in the 1920s. They were non-toxic – good news for industrial workers – non-flammable and highly stable. But this very stability was the cause of the problem, because they are not broken down until they reach the upper atmosphere and destroyed by the intensity of the sun's rays. So chlorine is released into the stratosphere, paving the way for the catalytic reactions which destroy ozone.
>
> (Tindale 1998: 57)

The consequences of such environmental changes are potentially catastrophic:

> Global warming is also implicated in the dramatic increase in what we used to term 'natural' disasters or 'acts of God'. The damage wrought by storms, floods, hurricanes and so on is spiralling upwards. In the first three years of the 1990s, there were twice as many major windstorms worldwide as in the whole of the 1980s, causing damage worth $20 billion.
>
> (Tindale 1998: 66)

The impact of modern science and technology, however, is not limited. The

Frankfurt school of sociologists has linked the exploitation of nature to the exploitation of individuals within modern society:

> The link between the domination of external nature and the domination of internal human nature was central to the thinking of the early Frankfurt School. Adorno and Horkheimer, condemning the Baconian determination to enable 'man to hold sway over a disenchanted nature', argue that the instrumental rationality which leads us to suppress the aesthetic, expressive and instinctive rationalities within ourselves leads us too to exploit the natural world.
>
> (Tindale 1998: 55)

In the twentieth century, attempts to engineer utopias whether on a micro scale, such as new housing estates, or on a macro scale, such as communist societies, have generally not succeeded and in some cases have resulted in major disasters. In particular, the attempts at creating new societies through social engineering such as Hitler's 'Final Solution' and Stalin's enforced collectivization in the 1930s not only resulted in large-scale loss of life but were ultimately unsuccessful. Historians are still analysing the scale of these man-made disasters. For example, Hobsbawm states that as a result of Stalin's actions the population of the Soviet Union in 1937 stood at 164 million, which was 16.7 million less than forecasted by the Second Five Year Plan (Hobsbawm 1994: 393). The comparisons historians make of the two disasters, however, indicate the limitations of Enlightenment thinking. Hitler's use of genocide to create a racially pure Aryan Reich is seen as both inhumane and irrational whereas Stalin's use of terror to modernize the Soviet Union is judged inhumane but rational (Kershaw and Lewin 1997).

In the twentieth century, the optimism of the utopia has been replaced by the pessimism of the dystopia, such as Orwell's vision in 1948 of *1984* modelled on his experiences of Soviet repression and the Second World War.

Some critics have argued that Hitler's final solution and Stalin's terror campaigns were not aberrations but are implicit within the whole Enlightenment endeavour. The Enlightenment rather than liberating *all* individuals, merely changed the pattern of repression. For example, feminists argue that the Enlightenment philosophers were all men who were concerned only with the rights of men. Thus the development of welfare services such as health care involved the medicalization of women's lives and bodies and subjugation to the dominant male doctor (for critical analysis see Harding 1997: 144). Enlightened reforms in the nineteenth century, such as the various Factory and Mine Acts which are usually seen as part of a civilizing process, reinforced patriarchal domination by excluding women from the productive process, restricting them to domestic labour and making them dependent on the male 'bread winner'.

Foucault is a major critic of the Enlightenment. He considered that the Enlightenment changed the pattern of oppression, developing a sophisticated technology of oppression. Prior to the Enlightenment, the oppression of marginal groups had been haphazard and the technologies, although brutal, such as the execution of regicides or the hanging of thieves, had been crude, unsophisticated public and external to the individual, punishment was

inflicted on the body. The Enlightenment was associated with the development of more 'civilized' and more sophisticated systems of control and
treatment such as prisons and mental hospitals that penetrated down to the
most basic level of society, right into the individual's mind and psyche, a
'governmentality'.

> Governmentality . . . which emerged in the eighteenth century, is an
> apparatus of security. This governmental apparatus required a whole
> series of specific *savoirs* (knowledges) and was the foundation for the rise
> of the administrative state . . . the whole development of psychology and
> psychiatry was seen in terms of forms of knowledge, relating to an
> extension of power over the subordinate populations of urban Europe.
>
> (Turner 1997: xiii)

These systems provided for total supervision and control and could be used
for mass domination. Just as it is possible to identify the origins of twentieth-
century totalitarian regimes such as Nazi Germany and the Stalinist Soviet
Union in the absolutist states of the eighteenth century, Frederick the Great's
Prussia (1740–86) and Catherine the Great's Russia (1762–96) (Anderson
1974), so it is possible to identify the origins of the technology of repression
and terror, the Nazi death camps which killed an estimated five and a half
million Jews and the Soviet Gulag Archipelago which killed an estimated
seventeen million Soviet citizens (Davies 1996: 1328–9) in the prisons and
mental hospitals of the nineteenth century.

Responding to the failures

The failures of science and technology have resulted in a rejection of the
Enlightenment endeavour to understand, control and improve nature and
society. The Indian writer Vandana Shiva summarizes this rejection:

> The act of living and conserving life in all its diversity – in people and in
> nature – seems to have been sacrificed to progress, and the sanctity of life
> has been substituted by the sanctity of science and development.
> Throughout the world, a new questioning is growing, rooted in the
> experience of those for whom the spread of what is called 'Enlightenment'
> has been the spread of darkness.
>
> (cited in Tindale 1998: 56)

This approach also underlies Illich's analysis of modern society. He argued
that such societies are characterized by the development of techno-bureau-
cracies. New technologies are created by experts and these technologies are
not only harmful but also disable individuals living in such societies. Thus in
modern societies individuals are exposed to the risk of expert-created hazards
such as iatrogenic or doctor-created disease (Illich 1976). Illich argued that the
only way to counteract the effects of modern technology is to return to
traditional or vernacular technology.

In contrast, Giddens believed that it is not only not feasible but also undesirable to turn back the clock. It is impossible because changes in the last 50
years have resulted in the 'end of nature' in so far as all aspects of nature are

affected by human activity and the 'end of tradition' in so far as human actions have an element of individual choice:

> To live after tradition is essentially to be in a world where life is no longer lived as fate. For many people – and this is still a source of class division in modern societies – diverse aspects of life were established by tradition as fate. It was the fate of a woman to be involved in a domestic milieu for much of her life, to have children and to look after the house . . . We no longer live our lives as fate, in a process which Ulrich Beck calls individualization . . . As customary ways of doing things become problematic, people must choose in many areas which used to be governed by taken-for granted norms. Eating is an example: there are no traditional diets any more.
>
> (Giddens 1990: 26 and 30)

It is undesirable because it reduces the collective and individual capacity to understand and manage risks and use them creatively. Thus for Giddens the way forward is to understand and manage risk more effectively:

> In a world where one can no longer simply rely on tradition to establish what to do in a given range of context, people have to take a more active and risk-infused orientation to their relationships and involvements.
>
> (Giddens 1990: 28)

The remainder of this chapter explores ways in which this can be done building on the insights generated by Parts 1, 2 and 3 of this book.

THE DEVELOPMENT OF HEALTH AND WELFARE SERVICES: TOWARDS REALISTIC UTOPIAS

In this section we explore the implications of the analysis of the development of a risk approach to the development of national policies for vulnerable individuals. This analysis will develop and build on the material presented in Part 1 of this book.

From an Enlightenment perspective, the history of the development of policies for vulnerable people should show certain characteristics. There should be evidence of:

- cumulation of knowledge about the causes of vulnerability and ways of managing it, resulting in
- improvements in services, from both improved technologies of care and treatment but also from more humane treatment of vulnerable individuals, implying
- progress not only of services but of the whole of society.

Viewed over a long time-frame, the history of policies does show some of the anticipated characteristics. In the pre-modern period there was very little knowledge or interest in the causes of vulnerability. Official interest was restricted to dealing with the effects of vulnerability and dangerousness. In

England statutes were not supported by any documents analysing the causes of the problems. Thus policy was essentially a restricted and pragmatic response to certain specific problems. The main focus of action was on maintaining the current structures of society, and there was little evidence of a 'humane' concern with the interests of vulnerable individuals. In so far as a pattern of 'policy development' or progress can be identified by comparing different statutes, it is a modern interpretation, mediaeval law-makers saw themselves as 'traditionalists' who were codifying existing customs and practices.

In contrast, policy formation in the modern period is characterized by a self-consciousness and a sense of change and development. For example, the liberal reforms of the early twentieth century were based on sustained analysis of the causes of different forms of vulnerability drawing on a range of 'scientific' research and expert opinion plus evaluation of alternative mechanisms for managing the problems created by vulnerable people (for a discussion of learning disability see Alaszewski, 1988). It is clear that policy makers sought to create structures which would provide for improved care and treatment and these were justified as being not only more effective but also more humane. In areas such as learning disability following the development of new policies, there was sustained investment in the new structures and practices (Alaszewski 1986). There is within the rhetoric of policy making a strong sense of progress, this often takes the form of comparing the unenlightened practices of the pre-reform period with the progressive practices which will develop as a result of the reforms.

However, a more detailed and fine-grained analysis of policy development in the modern period makes it difficult to sustain the view of progress and development. In particular, reforms and developments that are presented as enlightened and progressive at one stage in the development of policy, are subsequently portrayed as traditional and repressive. This is clear if the Liberal Reforms of the early twentieth century are compared with policy developments in the late twentieth century (see Chapter 2). Institutions such as Reformatory and Industrial Schools for children or Colonies and Hospitals for people with a learning disability were an important element of the Liberal Reforms. They presented as sources of knowledge, supposedly centres of humane and effective treatment and symbols of progress within a civilized society. By the 1960s, these same institutions were presented in a very different light. They were seen as intellectual backwaters, the staff in them needed retraining in 'modern' knowledge and practices. They were seen as old fashioned and traditional providing an institutional and inhumane form of treatment. The resources they consumed were a serious impediment to the development of more enlightened, progressive and humane forms of care and treatment.

The more fine-grained analysis of policy development in the modern period, especially when applied to specific groups of vulnerable clients, tends to indicate that there are oscillations or cycles within policy (Jones 1972). These cycles are associated with changes in knowledge and shifts in the perception of the policy issues. Thus within the development of mental health policy, it is possible to identify cycles of therapeutic optimism associated with new treatment regimes followed by periods of pessimism as the limitations or failures of the regimes become apparent.

At the beginning of the nineteenth century, revolutionary politics and the development of Enlightenment thinking was associated with the development of optimistic therapeutic 'moral treatment' regimes. As the asylum movement gathered pace in the mid-nineteenth century, so it became clear that moral treatment could not be sustained within the context of mass treatment, and therapeutic optimism was replaced by a 'pessimism of degeneracy' theory with the asylums warehousing 'untreatable' cases. The development of psychotherapy and the recognition of neurosis in the shell-shocked victims of the First World War, plus the exposure of conditions in the asylums was associated with the development of a limited optimism. If mental illness could be identified in the early stages, then treatment using new technologies was possible. Thus acute patients could be treated as voluntary patients using the new technologies, though chronic cases needed to be warehoused. The development of effective drug treatments in the 1950s and the sustained criticism of the old asylums opened up a new period of optimism. All patients could now be treated and the new drugs could be used to sustain and manage mental illness within the community. The mental hospitals could be shut and replaced by care in the community. There are signs that this wave of optimism is again giving place to a more pessimistic climate. High-profile incidents in which patients with enduring mental illness have seriously harmed themselves and others have led to more emphasis on control. Drug therapies may be effective in managing some of the symptoms of mental illness, but may not be effective in dealing with the underlying causes. Individuals with enduring problems may choose not to take their prescribed drugs because of side effects or dislike of medication. Thus there is a renewed move towards control, a slowing down of the hospital closure programme and the development of increased measures to control patients discharged from hospital (Goodwin 1997).

Underlying these fluctuations are movements between utopian optimism, in which there is a belief that an ideal society could be created, and negative realism in which the problems are seen as insolvable and the only response is the use of harsh measures to control them. Central to such shifts are perceptions of the capacity for individuals to sustain change, the utopias were based on the belief that the individuals could be reprogrammed. Rothman (1971) described this process in the Jacksonian reforms in the USA at the start of the of the nineteenth century. Rothman saw these reforms as a large-scale social experiment designed to create a model society by reprogramming problematic individuals such as criminals and the insane. Early colonists were not particularly concerned with causes of social problems such as insanity: 'The question of the etiology of insanity was a comparatively new one for Americans. The colonists assumed that its causes, like that of other diseases, rested with God's will' (Rothman 1971: 107).

In the early nineteenth century, the intellectual inspiration for the development of 'enlightened' policies came from Europe where Enlightenment thinking was underpinning large-scale social reform:

In the aftermath of the [American] Revolution, however, a spark of interest appeared, lit by Enlightenment ideology and an awareness of very dramatic events in Europe. Just as Beccaria had insisted that humane laws could eradicate crime, so men like Tuke in England and Pinel in France insisted that kind and gentle treatment would help to cure insanity. The image of Pinel freeing the insane from their chains at Saltpêtrière had an immediate and obvious appeal to men of the new republic.

(Rothman 1971: 197–8)

Experts in the USA such as doctors identified major problems within US society and used rational methods to identify the causes of social problems within contemporary society:

Medical superintendents were eager to cure mental illness, prodded on by Enlightenment doctrines and a faith in progress, and republican patriotism. Convinced that to identify the source of the problem would be to master it, they looked avidly for faults in society.

(Rothman 1971: 126)

Having identified the problems, dysfunctions within society, these experts then designed utopias which would provide therapeutic environments in which individuals could be changed and healed:

The institution itself held the secret to the cure of insanity . . . [they would] create a different kind of environment, which methodically corrected the deficiencies of the community, and a cure for insanity was at hand. This, in essence, was the foundation of the asylum solution and the programme that came to be known as moral treatment. The institution would arrange and administer a disciplined routine that would curb uncontrolled impulses without cruelty or unnecessary punishment. It would re-create fixity and stability to compensate for the irregularities of the society. Thus, it would rehabilitate the casualties of the system. The hospital walls would enclose a new world for the insane, designed in the reverse image to the one they had left . . . There was a utopian flavour to correctional institutions.

(Rothman 1971: 133)

However, as Rothman noted utopias failed: individuals placed within them often did not change in the desired manner. The optimism was replaced by pessimistic realism:

The insane asylum suffered the most drastic decline from a reform to a custodial operation. By 1870 both the reality of institutional care and the rhetoric of psychiatrists made clear that the optimism of reformers had been unfounded, and the expectation of eradicating insanity from the new world had been illusionary.

(Rothman 1971: 265)

One major cause of the problems in policy is that the starting point for the development of both policy and practice is usually conceptualized in terms of need. The concept of need is very much a product of the intellectual tradition of the Enlightenment in which the emphasis is on the individual as the basic unit of analysis and action. Thus the individual is seen as a unit which has positive attributes such as qualifications, wealth, health and negative attributes, such as ignorance, poverty and disease. These negative attributes or needs are often contrasted to some notional ideal and professional and agency action is aimed at attaining these ideals.

This approach has a number of obvious limitations. It is difficult to agree the baseline against which need is defined. There is a discounting of the social context of the individual. There is a tendency to universalize need. If an ideal standard is adopted then virtually everybody may be defined as having a need. In such a situation it becomes difficult to prioritize intervention and a random element enters into the allocation of services. Furthermore, it may be difficult to assess the success of an intervention as it can never meet all the needs of an individual.

Risk offers an alternative to need. Risk is based on an assessment of an individual or groups within a specific context and is based on considerations of vulnerability and potential harm and particularly on interventions which will minimize harm. Thus the approach does not start with any particular idea or assumptions about desirable conditions or behaviours. In a needs framework, behaviours such as the use of an illicit drug would automatically be seen as indicating a need and therefore professional intervention, and this intervention would require the individual to change his or her behaviour, i.e. to be reprogrammed. Such an approach can lead to a view that: 'It is not environmental factors, or bacteria or viruses per se that cause illness; the critical factors resides in individuals, more particularly their self control' (Nettleton 1997: 214).

In a risk framework, it is the potential harmful consequences of the behaviour rather than the behaviour itself which would form the focus of intervention. This creates the possibility of focused interventions which concentrate on harm reduction. Thus there is no automatic tendency towards intervention and the approach provides criteria for evaluating success, i.e. to what extent have accidents, incidents and harm been avoided. Used systematically, risk would give policy makers and service providers a more sophisticated understanding of the causes of health and social problems. For example, it would enable them to differentiate risks associated with possible intrinsic vulnerability of an individual with a learning disability, risk associated with individual behaviour such as drug misuse and risks associated with environmental hazards such as infectious disease. The approach also provides the basis for evaluating success, i.e. the extent to which accidents, incidents and harm have been prevented.

The harm minimization approach is probably best developed within drug policy. As Stimson pointed out, the impact of HIV/AIDS has resulted in a shift in drug policy from criminalization of all illicit drug use towards harm minimization, such as needle exchange schemes which imply a degree of toleration of drug use (Stimson 1990: 336). Harm reduction is becoming a major focus of alcohol and drugs policy (Des Jarlais *et al.* 1993, Reuter and Caulkins 1995, Single 1997 and Stimson and Thom 1997).

The advantages of harm reduction strategies are that they are essentially realistic and pragmatic both at a societal level and also at a 'street level'. At the societal level, it may be considered ideal to have a society free of illegal drugs but measures designed to create a drug free society such as prohibition tend to be unsuccessful and may create harm. The current prohibition of drugs is associated with a continued rise in drug use and in some areas, for example, cocaine use in the USA, appears to be out of control (Mugford 1991). Such approaches tend to create their own problems such as the development of an illicit criminalized market in drugs. Harm reduction strategies are 'bottom up' rather than 'top down' (Marlatt 1996). They seek to shape user behaviour by providing users with information and choice. Thus Marlatt argued they are both realistic and humane and therefore offer a better chance of success.

At 'street level', harm reduction improves the relationship between users and services facilitating better user access and greater understanding of service providers. By providing a low threshold of access to services (Marlatt 1996), harm reduction strategies facilitate contacts, providing support and oppor-tunities for individuals who wish to reduce their dependency. They also enhance communication between users and professionals. As Rhodes (1997) pointed out, risk and risk behaviour have become key concepts in policy debates about drugs, sex and AIDS. However, he argued that professional conceptions of risk are primarily derived from epidemiological work. Inter-ventions based on this type of evidence are limited because they fail to capture risk as understood and experienced by drug users. The development of harm reduction both implies a greater acceptance of user behaviour and through increased contact can foster a more sophisticated understanding and therefore more effective public health interventions.

Although harm reduction strategies are being promoted essentially for pragmatic reasons and as the 'least bad alternative' (Strang and Farrell 1992), it is also possible to identify a rational, even utopian element within them. They aim to create a better and a safer society by directly and immediately reducing harm and indirectly, in the longer term, reducing the overall inci-dence of harmful behaviours. They are rational in so far as they are concerned with identifying causes and basing interventions on analysis of the reasons for actions. However, unlike more idealistic approaches, they do not attempt to re-engineer the individual by taking away his or her choice to engage in behaviours such as alcohol consumption or illicit drug use, rather they are more concerned with identifying and changing the specific aspects of these behaviours that cause harm.

AGENCIES' STRATEGIES FOR MANAGING HEALTH AND WELFARE: UNCERTAINTY, PREDICTABILITY AND CONTROL

Enlightenment thinking not only shaped the ways in which society was studied, it also influenced the study of components of society such as organ-izations. This influence is particularly clearly marked in the classic sociological studies of Max Weber (see Chapters 3 and 4).

Weber used 'ideal' types to characterize different forms of organizations. He characterized them in terms of the cooperation that underpinned them, i.e.

why individuals felt they had to work together within the framework of the organization. He argued that in pre-modern or patriarchal societies, individuals' cooperation was based primarily on custom and practice based on the irrational elements such as fear of change and magic:

> The validity of a social order by virtue of the sacredness of tradition is the oldest and most universal type of legitimacy. The fear of magical evils reinforces the general psychological inhibitions against any sort of change in customary modes of action. At the same time the manifold vested interests which tend to favor conformity with an established order help to perpetuate it.
>
> (Weber 1968a: 37)

As European societies modernized in the eighteenth and nineteenth centuries, so 'traditional' organizations were replaced by modern organizational types, particularly bureaucracies. The bureaucracy can be seen as the ideal type of an Enlightenment organization based on knowledge and reason. Both influence bureaucracy in a number of ways. Bureaucracies are the product of human reason in that they have explicit and agreed goals and they have formal structures designed to achieve these goals. Their operating structures are rational as they ensure that decisions and actions are based on rational rules which are 'tried and proven'. The individual bureaucrat has the appropriate knowledge and skills to make rational decisions. They are appointed on the basis of formal qualification and experience:

> Bureaucratization offers above all the optimum possibility for carrying through the principle of specializing administrative functions according to purely objective considerations. Individual performances are allocated to functionaries who have specialized training and who by constant practice increase their expertise. 'Objective' discharge of business primarily means a discharge of business according to *calculable rules* 'without regard for persons.'
>
> (Weber 1968b: 975, original emphasis)

Weber, however, recognized that in both pre-modern and modern societies, organizations could develop spontaneously around the personal qualities of a charismatic leader. Central to this type of organization is the issue of trust, the leader selects individuals he or she trusts as a select inner group and supporters follow the leader because they trust his or her insight or vision:

> The charismatic hero derives his authority not from an established order and enactments, as if it were an official competence, and not from custom or feudal fealty, as under patrimonialism. He gains and retains it solely by proving his powers in practice . . . The mere fact of recognizing the personal mission of a charismatic master establishes his power. Whether it is more active or passive, this recognition derives from the surrender of the faithful to the extraordinary and unheard-of, to what is alien to all regulation and tradition and therefore is viewed as divine – surrender which arises from distress or enthusiasm. Hence, in a revolutionary and

sovereign manner, charismatic domination transforms all values and breaks all traditional and rational norms.

(Weber 1968b: 1114–5)

The contrast between the rule and order orientation of bureaucracy and the creativity and disorder of charisma has remained important in debates about organizational strategies. The rational rule-based organization seeks to impose order and control both on its environment and its internal processes. As we argued in Chapter 3, it is safety-oriented and risk averse. Weber himself recognized the cost of this approach. He argued that while bureaucracies were more efficient and would therefore replace organizations based on other principles, they also harmed individuals. They deprived 'bureaucrats' of the ability to fully express their humanity, imagination and creativity by placing them within an administrative 'iron cage'.

Bureaucracy develops the more perfectly, the more it is 'dehumanized,' the more completely it succeeds in eliminating from official business love, hatred, and all purely personal, irrational, and emotional elements which escape calculation. This is appraised as its special virtue by capitalism . . . The individual bureaucrat cannot squirm out of the apparatus into which he has been harnessed . . . The professional bureaucrat is chained to his activity in his entire economic and ideological existence. In the great majority of cases he is only a small cog in a ceaselessly moving mechanism which prescribes to him an essentially fixed route of march.

(Weber 1968b: 975 and 987–8)

As Gerth and Wright Mills noted, Weber was essentially a romantic who recognized the irresistible modernization of society through rational institutions such as bureaucracies but at the same time was aware of the damaging and dehumanizing aspects of this process:

Weber thus identifies bureaucracy with rationality, and the process of rationalization with mechanism, depersonalization, and oppressive routine. Rationally, in this context, is seen as adverse to personal freedom. Accordingly, Weber is a nostalgic liberal, feeling himself on the defensive. He deplores the type of man that the mechanization and the routine of bureaucracy selects and forms. The narrowed professional, publicly certified and examined, and ready for tenure and career.

(Gerth and Wright Mills 1947: 50)

There appears to be in modern society a choice in organizational designs between organizations which are rational and safe but whose products are unexciting but predictable, and those which emphasize creativity and imagination and produce exciting but less reliable products. Ritzer (1993) argued that the rational bureaucratic organization as characterized by McDonald's dominates modern society. Management gurus such as Tom Peters clearly wish to encourage managerial strategies that are liberating and 'chaotic' (1992a; 1992b). Peters has been particularly critical of the safety orientation which he believed dominates large-scale corporations in the USA:

With madness afoot in every marketplace, glory, I predict, will go to leaders in firms who attack the future with the most zest, the most tries, the most failures. This is the worst of all times to engage in perpetual analysis, and to run from risk, from action-taking – and mistakes . . . The pursuit of 'risk-free,' within the corporation, means answering any and all questions with 'no' or 'it depends' . . . those that pursue 'risk-free' by hiding behind regulations that delay action are doubtless putting themselves into the highest risk category.

(Peters 1992b: 584–5)

A similar analysis underpinned a motoring journalist's discussion of the effects of the take-over of a small innovative motor manufacturer, Saab, by a large conservative multi-national. In his view, it resulted in the replacement of an innovative and exciting car with a dull and unimaginative model:

'Beyond the conventional' proclaims Saab's motto. But in truth the 9–5 is extremely conventional: what it does is take convention and refine it, via computer-aided design and teamworking, to the nth degree of chilly perfection. It is not a risk-taking, but a risk-eliminating strategy.

(Seaton 1997: 52)

It appears in modern society that both individually and collectively a choice has to been made between rationality and creativity, sciences and arts or between safety and risk taking. For example, a doctor who decided to become a writer described his decision as choosing 'humanity over rationality' and the central theme of his first book is based on a solar eclipse in India and centres on the debate between modern rationality and traditional irrationality:

I was fascinated by the debate of science versus myth and how Indian rationalists were trying to counter their society's superstitions about how eclipses bring disastrous events. It struck a deep chord with my conflict between the science in medicine and the humanity of people. Although *Eclipse of the Sun* has nothing from my life in it, the book is deeply autobiographical! It has the two sides of my personality embodied in it, the husband is the scientist and the wife is spiritual. I set them against each other and allow them to tussle it out on the page. Neither side wins – although the science and the rational side comes off worse.

(Whitaker 1997: 18)

As we pointed out in Chapter 4, in safety-oriented organizations, individuals can and do disregard the dominant culture, indeed informal cultures can develop that are innovative but in such organizations these decisions are made and cultures exist despite the formal structure and individuals who take risks will be blamed if things go wrong.

The central issue in organizational design is whether it is possible to create an organization that is both ordered, i.e. safe and efficient, and at the same time disordered, i.e. allows for and encourages the randomness of individual creativity and inspiration. The only way to achieve this is to develop effective strategies for managing risk. Such strategies require a number of elements:

- an extended definition of risk;
- awareness of the risk implications of all aspects of organizational management;
- specification of the level and limits of trust.

An extended definition of risk
The problem with many organizations is that they utilize a narrow and 'common-sense' definition of risk. They are actually concerned with hazards rather than risk. A full definition of risk can only develop when both the positive and negative outcomes of decision making are identified and linked to each other in an assessment which includes an estimation of the probability of each type of outcome. If an organization only identifies hazards and does not seek to assess probability then its managerial processes and strategies will be cautious and defensive. Safety will be its dominant concern.

The use of an extended definition of risk shifts the focus from the identification of specific hazards to the process of decision making. As Carson (1994) argued a broader conception of risk leads to better decisions. This broader conception balances positive and negative outcomes with certainty and uncertainty:

> RISK AS DECISION MAKING: Risk-taking involves complex decision making. Different outcomes (which may be beneficial or harmful) with different values and likelihoods, each of which will vary over different risk periods and forms of risk management, have to be borne in mind, along with consideration of what is not known and how important this might be. A risk decision can only be as good as the decision maker and his or her methods.
>
> (Carson 1995: 27)

Extending the definition of risk also extends the role of front-line staff in welfare agencies. In the narrow definition, the formal role of front-line staff is to identify and respond to hazards. The broader definition extends their role to risk managers who can creatively use their knowledge and professional judgement to balance positive and negative outcomes and estimate probabilities so that the best decisions are made.

Towards total risk management
Agencies using a narrow definition of risk, tend to develop risk policies that are not only hazard-oriented but also treat the management of these hazards as separate from and distinctive from other aspects of management. The responsibility for this hazard-orientation is blamed on external pressure and it is implied that the agency has no choice in the matter. This can be seen in the following policy developed by a charity providing care and support for people with a learning disability:

> RISK ASSESSMENT   *Background*   The Health and Safety at Work Act 1974 stipulates that where an undertaking employs 5 or more persons at a location, then risk assessment must be completed . . . The original

conception of HSW was industrial and some of the regulations do not sit comfortably in a care setting.

This 'external pressure' is used to justify a policy that concentrates entirely on hazards management:

> *The Approach*   The start point is the identification of something with the potential to cause harm. This can include substances, machines, methods of work or other aspects of work organisation. This is known as a HAZARD. The likelihood that the harm from a particular hazard is realised is known as the RISK. The risk, therefore, reflects both the likelihood that harm will occur and its severity (emphasis in the original).

However, as we pointed out in Chapter 3, organizations can and do make choices. For example, they can choose whether to have a blameist or absolutionist policy. This has implications not only for risk policy and decisions but for all aspects of decision making and therefore other policies such as personnel need to be congruent with the risk policy. If agencies wish to have a broader and more open policy towards risk, risk issues should not be ghettoized in risk policies, but should underpin all aspects of organizational policies and agencies need to move towards total risk management orienting all management systems towards effective risk management.

Conditional trust

Underpinning the effective strategies of risk management is the issue of trust. Trust is both the cement of relationships and the lubricant of interaction between the public, the welfare agency and its front-line staff. The public trusts agencies to protect them both as anonymous members of the public and as potential or known users of the agency services. The front-line worker is trusted by both the agency and by the user to deliver appropriate care and support. Front-line workers have to trust their organization to protect them from the hazards involved in providing care and support. Trust in many ways is a pre-modern concept. As is clear from dictionary definitions, it involves faith or belief:

> *trust*   1. Firm belief in the honesty, veracity, justice, strength, etc., of a person or thing . . .   2. Reliance on the truth of statement, etc. without examination . . .   7. Thing, person committed to one's care . . .
> (*Concise Oxford Dictionary* 1964)

In traditional societies, founded on face-to-face relationships, trust was based on personal knowledge that individuals had of each other and more general information such as reputation. As Giddens (1990) pointed out, strangers were unknown and therefore distrusted. However, in modern society, transactions involving highly sensitive and potentially damaging information which can have a major impact on an individual's life, such as the diagnosis of a disease, often take place between strangers. Encounters between professionals and clients are often anonymous, involve complex and abstract issues and may involve threats either generated by the encounter or by the professional:

The reliance placed by lay actors upon expert systems is not just a matter – as was normally the case in the pre-modern world – of generating a sense of security about an independently given universe of events. It is a matter of the calculation of benefit and risk in circumstances where expert knowledge does not just provide that calculus but actually *creates* (or reproduces) the universe of events, as a result of the continual reflexive implementation of that very knowledge.

(Giddens 1990: 84)

It is possible to deal with such encounters by treating them as if they were based on traditional face-to-face relationships. For example, in the British National Health Service, general medical practitioners are called 'family practitioners' and there is an implication that they will have a personal knowledge of each member of the family. Often it is not possible to build up personalized knowledge between between client and professional and some specific action needs to be taken to ensure trust is maintained:

Encounters with the representatives of abstract systems, of course, can be regularised and may easily take on characteristics of trustworthiness associated with friendship and intimacy. This may be the case, for example, with a doctor, dentist or travel agent dealt with regularly over a period of years. However, many encounters with the representatives of abstract systems are more periodic or transitory than this. Irregular encounters are probably those in which the evidential criteria of reliability have to be especially carefully laid out and protected, although such criteria are also displayed in the whole range of lay-professional encounters.

(Giddens 1990: 85)

Coote argued that this trust can be developed through a genuine commitment by health and welfare agencies to democracy and the involvement of lay people in strategic decision making:

The mutual respect which is integral to an adult-to-adult relationship implies a degree of trust in the other. Not blind faith, but the kind of measured confidence that comes from informed understanding. Trust has broken down because politics is characterized by secrecy, spin-doctoring and special pleading. We can only rebuild it by moving forwards, not backwards. There are two backward-looking strategies which some have adopted as ways of dealing with the new mood of insecurity . . . A high-trust democracy is built on understanding and consensus not on instruction and obedience.

(Coote 1998: 126)

Although Coote defined her realistic utopia as 'high trust democracy', she saw the relationship between the public, agency and front-line workers in terms of conditional trust or 'measured confidence'. This conditional confidence would mean, for example, that agencies supported their front-line workers and users trusted them, as long as such workers acted in good faith. Therefore there need to be safeguards which provide evidence that practitioners are acting in good faith. The Clothier report points to the problems created by a single untrustworthy practitioner and the lack of safeguards in one particular hospital:

> We were struck throughout our Inquiry by the way in which fragments of medical evidence which, if assembled, would have pointed to Allitt as the malevolent cause of the unexpected collapses of children, lay neglected or were missed . . . The principal failure of those concerned lay in not collecting together those pieces of evidence. The initiative and energy needed to do this were not forthcoming at [the hospital]. That is the true and ultimate criticism. Civilised society has very little defence against the aimless malice of a deranged mind. Wherever we have found the slightest possibility of prevention, we have pointed to it. The tightening of standards which we have sometimes urged must be a good in itself and such small improvements may reduce the opportunities open to another Beverly Allitt.
>
> (Clothier 1994: 131)

The trust of the public can be enhanced by greater agency openness but ultimately it is conditional on confidence in practitioner decision making and it is to this issue we turn in the next section.

THE DILEMMAS OF PROFESSIONAL PRACTICE: KNOWLEDGE, VALUES AND DECISIONS

Although some of the established professions can trace their origins back to pre-modern organizations such as mediaeval guilds, the development of modern professions was influenced by Enlightenment thinking in a number of ways. Underpinning the professional endeavour is a commitment to modernization and scientific rationality, the collection and application of knowledge to generate social progress by improving control of nature and social relations. Parsons described one area of professional practice in the following way:

> Modern medical practice is organized about the application of scientific knowledge to the problems of illness and health, to the control of 'disease' . . . modern medical practice is organized about the application of scientific knowledge by technically competent, trained personnel.
>
> (Parsons 1951: 431 and 454)

Since Parsons defined illness as a disturbance of normal human functioning resulting from a disruption of an individual's biological system and/or from his or her personal and social relations, the scope of the medical practitioner is broad.

At the high point of professional development, which in Britain was the immediate post-war period, there was unconditional trust by both politicians and the public in professional decision making and professional judgement. Thus the growth of the welfare state in the 1950s involved not only the substantial growth of public expenditure on health and welfare but the delegation of control of this expenditure to professional groups. Since the 1950s there has been a loss of confidence in them, especially by the state. The inexorable rise of state expenditure on welfare and the recessions of the 1980s have placed a strain on the relationship between the state and professionals and there is no longer a willingness to trust professional decision making and judgements.

There are concerns about the quality of professional decision making both in terms of its outcome and in terms of the processes used. In terms of outcomes, there is evidence of variability and error. Clinicians presented with the same information make different decisions:

> The conceptually separable questions of *how* clinicians make judgments and decisions and of *how well* they make them have both become of greater interest to a wide range of parties, the evaluative question being the dominant concern of those who see themselves as bearing the costs, monetary or personal, of inferior judgments and decisions. The wide variation in clinical practices uncovered by virtually all studies of clinical behaviour – whether the comparison is between colleagues, communities or countries – has been one of empirical focus for those attempting to assess professional performance. The significant percentage of discrepancies between clinical diagnoses and pathological findings which emerges in most autopsy studies is another.
>
> (Dowie and Elstein 1988: 2)

The government's response to this evidence has been to seek to develop more systematic decision making. In the National Health Service, this has involved the development of clinical guidelines and the use of evidence-based practice. This move to greater central control of professional decision making underpins the Labour Government's White Paper on the NHS. The aims of the reforms are set very much within an Enlightenment framework, with an emphasis on the need to change and modernize to create progress:

> The NHS cannot stand still. It needs to modernise if it is to meet patients' aspirations for up-to-date, quicker, more responsive services. The White Paper sets out an ambitious and far reaching programme of modernisation.
>
> (Department of Health 1997b)

Central to this programme of modernization is the collection and use of scientific knowledge as the basis of decision making to ensure the most effective and efficient delivery of health care. In the White Paper three separate mechanisms are identified to ensure knowledge is used in the NHS:

1 National standards and guidelines through new evidence-based National Service Frameworks to help ensure consistent access to services and quality of care right across the country.
2 A new National Institute for Clinical Excellence to give a strong lead on clinical and cost effectiveness, drawing up new guidelines from the latest scientific evidence.

3 A new organization to tackle shortcomings: a new Commission for Health Improvement will support and oversee the quality of clinical services locally, and will tackle shortcomings.

(Department of Health 1997b)

This approach emphasized the importance of knowledge but it failed to address directly the issue of decision making. To achieve better outcomes, practitioners need to use information effectively. Eddy argued that practitioners should handle the uncertainty of decision making more effectively by using decision-support techniques:

Over the past few hundred years languages have developed for collecting and interpreting evidence (statistics), dealing with uncertainty (probability theory), synthesizing evidence and estimating outcomes (mathematics), and making decisions (economics and decision theory). These languages are not currently learned by most clinical policymakers; they should be.

(Eddy 1998: 58)

This approach would enhance the technical competence of practitioners but it would not necessarily ensure that the decisions were sensitive to the specific circumstance of each case. As we showed in Chapter 6, clinical decisions are made in relationship to specific clients. They relate to the unique characteristics of each case and often involve issues of values, especially when there is tension between different interests in the decision-making process. More 'general' technical knowledge will not necessarily assist with the unique case and it will certainly not resolve conflicts of values.

The technocratic solutions threaten to make professionals into rule-following bureaucrats, and there is a danger that in rejecting this approach individual practitioners will see the only alternative as a rule-breaking, charismatic and idiosyncratic clinician using his or her personal experience and intuition to make clinical judgements. However, Schön identified an alternative approach, called reflective practice, in which an individual practitioner can systematically interpret and understand a situation:

When a practitioner reflects in and on his practice, the possible objects of his reflection are as varied as the kinds of phenomena before him and the systems of knowing-in-practice which he brings to them. He may reflect on the tacit norms and appreciation which underlie a judgment, or on the strategies and theories implicit in a pattern of behavior . . . When the phenomenon at hand eludes the ordinary categories of knowledge-in-practice, presenting itself as unique or unstable, the practitioner may surface and criticize his initial understanding of the phenomenon, construct a new description of it, and test the new description by an on-the-spot experiment. Sometimes he arrives at a new theory of the phenomenon by articulating a feeling he has about it.

(Schön 1988: 72)

The reflective practitioner who has a broad and sophisticated understanding of risk and the ability to understand and manage it, minimizes harm and maximizes benefit. Such a practitioner would merit the trust of both his or her agency, the users of his or her services and the public.

THE RISK OF RISK: A FINAL COMMENT

It is clear that risk is central to health and welfare services in late modern society. Effective management of risk can enhance social welfare and contribute to the more efficient use of resources and to a more equitable society. Effective management requires a broad definition of risk, realistic harm minimization policies, open agency policies based on conditional trust and reflective decision-making by practitioners. Narrow definitions of risk, associated with pessimistic policies and defensive agency policy plus unreflective practice will result in a more intrusive and repressive health and welfare system based on mistrust and compulsion. As one nurse in our research study put it: 'We should not let our uncertainties allow us to abuse people – that's the danger, life is a risk.'

BIBLIOGRAPHY

Alaszewski, A. (1986) *Institutional Care and the Mentally Handicapped: The Mental Handicap Hospital*. London: Croom Helm.

Alaszewski, A. (1988) From villains to victims: a short history of changes in attitudes in official policy, in A. Leighton (ed.) *Mental Handicap in the Community*. Cambridge: Woodhead-Faulkner.

Alaszewski, A. (1994) Restructuring health and welfare professions in the UK: the impact of internal markets on the medical, nursing and social work professions, in T. Johnson, G. Larkin and M. Saks (eds) *Health Professions and the State in Europe*. London: Routledge.

Alaszewski, A. (1995) Restructuring health and welfare professions in the UK, in T. Johnson, G. Larking and M. Saks (eds) *Health Professions and the State in Europe*. London: Routledge.

Alaszewski, H., Alaszewski, A. and Ayer, S. (1997) Teaching and learning about risk, Working Paper, Institute of Health Studies, University of Hull.

Alaszewski, A. and Dodson, G. (1991) Real lives: Dylan's story, *Social Work Today*, 23, 14–15.

Alaszewski, A. and Harrison, L. (1988) Collaboration and co-ordination between welfare agencies: a literature review, *British Journal of Social Work*, 18, 635–47.

Alaszewski, A., Harrison, L., Manthorpe, J. and Walsh, M. (1997) Managing risk in the city: the role of welfare professionals in managing risks from vulnerable individuals in cities, *Health and Place*, 3, 15–23.

Alaszewski, A. and Manthorpe, J. (1991) Measuring and managing risk in social welfare, *British Journal of Social Work*, 21, 277–90.

Alaszewski, A. and Manthorpe, J. (1998) Welfare agencies and risk: the missing link? *Health and Social Care in the Community*, 6 (1): 4–15.

Alaszewski, A. and Ong, B. N. (eds) (1990) *Normalisation in Practice: Residential Care for Children with a Profound Mental Handicap*. London: Routledge.

Alaszewski, A. and Walsh, M. (1995) Typologies of welfare organizations: a literature review, *British Journal of Social Work*, 25, 805–15.

Aldridge, M. (1994) *Making Social Work News*. London: Routledge.

Anderson, P. (1974) *Lineages of the Absolutist State*. London: NLB.

Anlau, S. (1992) The professionalization of social work: a case study of three organizational settings, *Sociology*, 26: 1–43.

Armstrong, D., Galloway, D. and Tomlinson, S. (1993) The assessment of special educational needs and the proletarianisation of professionals, *British Journal of Sociology of Education*, 14, 399–408.

Attenborough, F. L. (ed., trans.) (1922) *The Laws of the Earliest English Kings*. Cambridge: Cambridge University Press.

Ayto, J. (1990) *Dictionary of Word Origins*. London: Bloomsbury.

Beck, U. (1992) *Risk Society: Towards a New Modernity*. London: Sage.

Beck, U. (1998) Politics of risk society, in J. Franklin (ed.) *The Politics of Risk Society*. Cambridge: Polity Press.

Beder, S. (1991) The fallible engineer, *New Scientist*, 2, 38–42.

Belknap, I. (1956) *Human Problems of a State Mental Hospital*. New York: McGraw-Hill.

Bernstein, P. L. (1996) *Against the Gods: The Remarkable Story of Risk*. New York: John Wiley.

Beynon, H. (1973) *Working for Ford*. London: Allen Lane and Penguin Education.

Billis, D. (1984) *Welfare Bureaucracies: Their Design and Change in Response to Social Problems*. London: Heinemann.

Blau, P. M. (1963) *The Dynamics of Bureaucracy*, (2nd edn). Chicago: University of Chicago Press.

Blau, P. M. and Meyer, M. N. (eds) (1971) *Bureaucracy in Modern Society*, (2nd edn). New York: Random House.

Bloch, M. (1961) *Feudal Society*, L. A. Manyon (trans). London: Routledge and Kegan Paul.

Bosk, C. L. (1988) Forgive and remember: managing medical failure, in J. Dowie and A. Elstein (eds) *Professional Judgment: A Reader in Clinical Decision Making*, Cambridge: Cambridge University Press.

Boyd, W. (chair) (1996) *Report of the Confidential Inquiry into Homicides and Suicides by Mentally Ill People*. London: Royal College of Psychiatrists.

Brandon, M., Lewis, A. and Thoburn, J. (1996) The Children Act definition of 'significant harm' – interpretation in practice, *Health and Social Care in the Community*, 4, 11–20.

Brearley, C. P. (1982) *Risk and Social Work*. London: Routledge and Kegan Paul.

Brewer, L. (1996) Bureaucratic organization of professional labor, *Australian and New Zealand Journal of Sociology*, 32, 21–38.

Britton (1865) F. M. Nichols (ed. and trans.), 2 vols. Oxford: Clarendon Press.

Brown, A. L. (1992) *The Governance of Late Medieval England 1272–1461*. London: Edward Arnold.

Burgess, D. W. (1996) personal communication.

Burns, T. R. and Stalker, G. M. (1961) *The Management of Innovation*. London: Tavistock.

Butler-Sloss, Lord Justice (1988) *Report of the Inquiry into Child Abuse in Cleveland*, Cm. 412. London: HMSO.

Carson, D. (1994) Dangerous people: through a broader conception of 'risk' and 'danger' to better decisions, *Expert Evidence*, 3, 51–69.

Carson, D. (1995) Calculated risk, policy: risk management, *Community Care*, Oct.–Nov., 26–7.

Carson, R. (1962) *Silent Spring*. London: Hamish Hamilton.

Chambers English Dictionary (1990) C. Schwarz (ed.). Edinburgh: Chambers.

Chatterton, M. (1975) 'Organisational Relationships and Processes in Police Work'. Dissertation, University of Manchester, Department of Sociology.

Checkland, P. B. (1981) *Systems Thinking, Systems Practice*. Chichester: Wiley.

Children Act (1908) *An Act to Consolidate and Amend the Law Relating to the Protection of Children and Young Persons, Reformatory and Industrial Schools, and Juvenile Offenders, and Otherwise to Amend the Law with respect to Children and Young Persons*, 8 Edward VII, CHAPTER 67.

Children Act (1989) 37 and 38 Elizabeth II, CHAPTER 41.

Clark, B. (1966) Organizational adaptation to professionals, in H. Vollmer and D. Mills (eds). *Professionalization*. Englewood Cliffs, NJ: Prentice Hall.

Clothier, C. (1994) *The Allitt Inquiry: Independent Inquiry Relating to Deaths and Injuries on the Children's Ward at Grantham and Kesteven General Hospital*. HMSO, London.

Lord Clyde (1992) *The Report of the Inquiry into the Removal of Children from Orkney in February 1991*. Edinburgh: HMSO.

Cook, G. (1996) Risk taking in rehabilitative care: professional and legal considerations', *Health Care in Later Life*, 1, 4–13.

Coote, A. (1998) Risk and public policy: towards a high-trust democracy, Franklin J. (ed.) *The Politics of Risk Society*. Cambridge: Polity Press.

Crossland, Sir Bernard (1992) Estimating engineering risk, in The Royal Society (ed.), *Risk: Analysis, Perception and Management*, Report of a Royal Society Study Group. London: The Royal Society.

Coulshed, V. (1990) *Management in Social Work*, London: Macmillan.

Council of Europe (1989) *Council Directive of 12.6.1989 on the Introduction of Measures to Encourage Improvements in the Safety and Health of Workers at Work*, 89/391/EEC. Brussels: Council of Europe.

Davies, N. (1996) *Europe: A History*. Oxford: Oxford University Press.

Department of Health (1988) *Protecting Children, A Guide for Social Workers Undertaking a Comprehensive Assessment*. London: HMSO.

Department of Health (1989a) *Caring for People: Community Care in the Next Decade and Beyond*, Cm. 848. London: HMSO.

Department of Health (1989b) *An Introduction to the Children Act*. London: HMSO.

Department of Health (1992) *The Health of the Nation: A Strategy for Health in England*. London: HMSO.

Department of Health (1992) *The Health of the Nation: A Strategy for Health in England*, Cm 1986, London: HMSO.

Department of Health (1995) *Child Protection: Messages from Research*. London: HMSO.

Department of Health (1996) *Building Bridges: A Guide to Arrangements for Inter-agency Working for the Protection of Severely Mentally Ill People*. London: Department of Health.

Department of Health (1997a) New powers for action against inefficient doctors, Press Release, 97/104, 20 May. London: Department of Health.

Department of Health (1997b) *The New NHS*, Cm. 3807. London: HMSO.

Department of Health and Social Security (1982) *Child Abuse: A Study of Inquiry Reports, 1973–1981*. London: HMSO.

Department of Health and Social Security (1985) *Government Response to the Second Report from the Social Services Committee 1984/85 Session: Community Care with Special Reference to Adult Mentally Ill and Mentally Handicapped People*. Cmnd 9674, HMSO, London.

Department of Health, The Scottish Office and the Welsh Office (1996) *The Obligations of Care*. London: HMSO.

Department of Health and Social Security and Welsh Office (1971) *Better Services for the Mentally Handicapped*, Cmd 4683. London: HMSO.

de Schweinitz, K. (1947) *England's Road to Social Security 1349 to 1947*. London: Oxford University Press.

Des Jarlais, D., Friedman, S. R. and Ward, T. P. (1993) Harm reduction: A public health response to the AIDS epidemic among injecting drug users, *Annual Review of Public Health*, 14, 413–50.

Dingwall, R. (1989) Some problems about predicting child abuse and neglect, Stevenson, O. (ed.) *Child Abuse: Public Policy and Professional Practice*. Hemel Hempstead: Harvester Wheatsheaf.

Dobos, C. (1992) Defining risk from the perspective of nurses in clinical roles, *Journal of Advanced Nursing*, 17, 1303–9.

Doll, R. and Peto, R. (1994) Mortality in relation to smoking: 40 years' observations on male British doctors, *British Medical Journal*, 309, 901–11.

Donaldson, L. G. (1982) R v City of Birmingham District Council, Ex. Parte O, *All England Law Reports*, 2, 356–69.

Douglas, M. (1986) *Risk Acceptability According to the Social Sciences*. London: Routledge and Kegan Paul.

Douglas, M. (1992) *Risk and Blame: Essays in Cultural Theory*. London: Routledge.

Dowie, J. and Elstein, A. (eds) (1988) *Professional Judgment: A Reader in Clinical Decision Making*. Cambridge: Cambridge University Press.

Dunningham, C. and Norris, C. (1995) A risky business: exchange, bargaining and risk in the recruitment and running of informers by English Police Officers, Paper presented at 47th Annual Conference of the American Society of Criminology, Boston USA, 14–18 November.

Eddy, D. M. (1998) Quality assurance and care, in R. Ellis (ed.) *Professional and Quality Assurance in the Caring Professions*. London: Croom Helm/Chapman Hall.

Edgerton, R. B. (1967) *The Cloak of Competence*. Berkeley, CA: University of California Press.

Edward I (1278) *Several Tenants Against Whom an Action of Waste is Maintainable*, 6 Edward I, CAP V.

Edward I (1285a) *Fresh Suit Shall be Made after Felons and Robberies from Town to Town*, 13 Edward I, Stat 2, CAP I.

Edward I (1285b) *Inquiry of Felons and Robbers, and the Country shall Answer if They be not Taken*, 13 Edward I, Stat 2, CAP II.

Edward I (1300) *Escheators Shall Commit no Waste in Wards Lands*, 28 Edward I, CAP XVIII.

Edward II (1324) *His Prerogative in the Custody of Lands of Idiots*, 17 Edward II, CAP IX.

Edward III (1349) *The Statutes of Labourers*, 23 Edward III, CAP I–VIII.

Elizabeth I (1601) *Act for the Relief of the Poor*, 43 Elizabeth I, CAP II.

Etzioni, A. (1964) *Modern Organizations*. Englewood Cliffs, NJ: Prentice Hall.

Evans-Pritchard, E. E. (1937) *Witchcraft, Oracles and Magic among the Azande*. Oxford: Clarendon Press.

Fennell, P. (1996) *Treatment without Consent: Law, Psychiatry and the Treatment of Mentally Disordered People since 1945*. London: Routledge.

Fleta (1984) G. O. Sayles (ed. and trans.), 4 vols. London: Selden Society.

Fox-Harding, L. (1991) *Perspectives in Child Care Policy*. London: Longman.

Gerth, H. H. and Wright Mills, C. (1947) (eds), *From Max Weber: Essays in Sociology*. London: Kegan Paul, Trench, Trubner.

Giddens, A. (1990) *The Consequences of Modernity*. Cambridge: Polity Press.

Giddens, A. (1991) *Modernity and Self-Identity: Self and Society in the Late Modern Age*. Cambridge: Polity Press.

Giddens, A. (1993) *Sociology*, 2nd edn. Cambridge: Polity Press.

Giddens, A. (1994) Agenda Change, *New Society and Statesman*, 7 October 1994, 23–5.

Goffman, E. (1961) *Asylums: Essays on the Social Situation of Mental Patients and Other Inmates*. New York: Doubleday Anchor.

Goodwin, S. (1997) *Comparative Mental Health Policy: From Institutional to Community Care*. London: Sage.

Green, A. D. (1966) The professional worker in the bureaucracy, *Social Services Review*, 40, 71–83.

Guy, P. (1994) A general social work council – a critical look at the issues. *British Journal of Social Work*, 24, 261–71.

Harding, A. (1966) *A Social History of English Law*. Harmondsworth: Penguin.

Harding, J. (1997) Bodies at risk: sex, surveillance and hormone replacement therapy, in A. Petersen and R. Bunton (eds) *Foucault, Health and Medicine*, London: Routledge.

Harrison, L., Tether, P. and Baggott, R. (1990) Regulation, in C. Godfrey and D. Robinson (eds) *Manipulating Consumption: Information, Law and Voluntary Controls*. Aldershot: Avebury.

Hawking, S. W. (1988) *A Brief History of Time: From the Big Bang to Black Holes*. London: Bantam Press.

Hay, J. R. (1983) *The Origins of the Liberal Welfare Reforms 1906–1914*, revd edn. Basingstoke: Macmillan.

Health and Safety at Work Act (1974) 22 and 23 Elizabeth II, CHAPTER 37.

Helman, C. (1984) Feed a cold, starve a fever, in N. Black *et al.* (eds) *Health and Disease: A Reader*. Milton Keynes: Open University Press.

Henry III (1225a) *The Wardship of an Heir within Age. The Heir a Knight*, 9 Henry III, CAP III.

Henry III (1225b) *No Waste shall be made by a Guardian in Wards Lands*, 9 Henry III, CAP IV.

Henry III (1225c) *Guardians shall maintain the Inheritance of their Wards: and of Bishopricks*, 9 Henry III, CAP V.

Henry III (1225d) *Heirs shall be married without Disparagement*, 9 Henry III, CAP VI.

Henry III (1235) *The Penalties for Ravishment of a Ward, Forfeiture of Marriage, or Disparagement of a Ward*, 20 Henry III, CAP VI.

Henry VIII (1530) *An Act Directing how Aged, Poor and Impotent Persons, Compelled to Live by Alms, shall be Ordered, and Vagabonds and Beggars shall be Punished*, 22 Henry VIII, CAP IV.

Heywood, J. (1978) *Children in Care: The Development of the Service for the Deprived Child*, 3rd edn. London: Routledge and Kegan Paul.

Hill, M. (1990) The manifest and latent lessons of child abuse inquiries, *British Journal of Social Work*, 20, 197–213.

Hobsbawm, E. (1994) *Age of Extremes: The Short Twentieth Century, 1914–1991*. London: Michael Joseph.

Home Office, Department of Health, Department of Education and Science and Welsh Office (1991) *Working Together Under the Children Act 1989 (A Guide to Arrangements for Inter-agency Co-operation for the Protection of Children from Abuse)*. London: HMSO.

Hood, C. C., Jones, D. K. C., Pidgeon, N. F., Turner, B. A. and Gibson, R. (1992) Risk management, in The Royal Society (ed.) *Risk, Analysis, Perception and Management: Report of a Royal Society Study Group*, The Royal Society, London.

Horrocks, P. (1989) The right not to be abused; taking risks and the safety of patients, in Age Concern Scotland (ed.) *Rights, Risks and Responsibilities*, Proceedings of the Conference held on 10 March, 1989 at St Andrew's College of Education, Age Concern Scotland.

House of Commons (1985) Second Report from the Social Services Committee, Sessions 1984–85, *Community Care, with Special Reference to Adult Mentally Ill and Mentally Handicapped People*, Vol. 1. London: HMSO.

Howe, D. (1992) Child abuse and the bureaucratization of social work, *Sociological Review*, 40, 491–508.

Hunt, G. (1995) (ed.) *Whistleblowing in the Health Service*. London: Edward Arnold.

Illich, I. D. (1976) *Limits to Medicine: Medical Nemesis, the Expropriation of Health*. London: Marion Boyars.

Jackson, M. (1991) *System Methodology for Management Sciences*. New York: Plenum.

Jackson, S., Sanders, R. and Thomas, N. (1995) 'Setting Priorities in Child Protection:

Perception of Risk and Agency Strategy', Paper read at the ESRC 'Risk in Organisational Settings' Conference, Regent's Park, London.

Jones, K. (1972) *A History of the Mental Health Services*. London: Routledge and Kegan Paul.

Jones, W. (1996) Seeking permission to treat, *NHS Magazine*, Spring, 18.

Kane, P. (1998) There's method in the magic, in J. Franklin (ed.) *The Politics of Risk Society*. Cambridge: Polity Press.

Kemshall, H. (1996) Offender risk and probation practice, in H. Kemshall and J. Pritchard (eds) *Good Practice in Risk Assessment and Risk Management*. London: Jessica Kingsley.

Kershaw, I. and Lewin, M. (1997) *Stalinism and Nazism: Dictatorships in Comparison*. Cambridge: Cambridge University Press.

King, M. (1995) Law's healing of children's hearing: the paradox moves north, *Journal of Social Policy*, 24 (3), 315–40.

King, R. D., Raynes, N. V. and Tizard, J. (1971) *Patterns of Residential Care*. London: Routledge and Kegan Paul.

Lawrie, C. (1997) Risk: the role and responsibilities of middle managers, in H. Kemshall and J. Pritchard (eds) *Good Practice in Risk Assessment and Risk Management 2: Protection, Rights and Responsibilities*. London: Jessica Kingsley.

Layfield, F. (1987) *Sizewell B. Public Enquiry: Summary of Conclusions and Recommendations*. London: HMSO.

Lichtenstein, S., Slovic, P., Fischhoff, B., Layman, M. and Combs, B. (1978) Judged frequency of lethal events, *Journal of Experimental Psychology (Human Learning and Memory)*, 4: 551–78.

Light, D. (1995) Countervailing powers: a framework for professions in transition, in T. Johnson, G. Larkin and M. Saks (eds) *Health Professions and the State in Europe*. London: Routledge.

MacAndrew, C. and Edgerton, R. (1964) The everyday life of institutionalised idiots, *Human Organization*, 23, 312–18.

Maine, H. J. S. (1866) *Ancient Law*, 3rd edn. London: John Murray.

Maitland, F. (1891) Notes and Documents, The 'Praerogativa Regis', *English Historical Review*, VI (XXII), 367–72.

Manning, P. K. (1977) *Police Work*. Cambridge, MA: MIT Press.

Mansell, J. L. (Chair) (1993) *Services for People with Learning Disabilities and Challenging Behaviour or Mental Health Needs*. London: HMSO.

Manthorpe, J. and Alaszewski, A. (1997) All societies need to allocate blame when disasters occur, *Community Care*, 19, 30 Oct.–5 Nov.

Manthorpe, J. and Alaszewski, A. (1998) Special issue on risk: editorial, *Health and Social Care in the Community*, 6 (1): 1–3.

Manthorpe, J. and Bradley, G. (1997) Developing a risk policy: the first phase, *Research, Policy and Planning*, 15 (1): 8–12.

Manthorpe, J. and Walsh, M., Alaszewski, A. and Harrison, L. (1997) Issues of risk, practice and welfare in learning disability services, *Disability and Society*, 12, 69–82.

Marlatt, G. A. (1996) Harm reduction: come as you are, *Addictive Behaviors*, 21, 779–88.

Marris, C., Langford, I. and O'Riordan, T. (1996) A comparison and integration of the psychometric and cultural theory approaches to risk perceptions, Paper read at the ESRC Risk and Human Behaviour Conference, Goodricke College, University of York, 18–20 September.

Marx, K. and Engels, F. (1962) *Selected Works in Two Volumes, Vol. 1*. Moscow: Foreign Languages Publishing House.

May, L. (1996) I do not believe most patients are in it for money: litigation, *NHS Magazine*, 4, Spring, 17–19.

McKinlay, J. B. (1975) Clients and organisations, in J. B. McKinlay (ed.) *Processing People: Cases in Organisational Behaviour*. London: Holt, Reinhart and Winston.

Mental Deficiency Act (1913) *An Act to make Further and Better Provision for the Care of Feeble-minded and other Mentally Defective Persons and to Amend the Lunacy Acts*, 3 and 4 George V, CHAPTER 28.

Mental Health Act (1983) 31 and 32 Elizabeth II, CHAPTER 20.

Miller, D. and Reilly, J. (1994) *Food 'Scares' in the Media*, Glasgow University Media Group, in association with the MRC Medical Sociology Unit, Glasgow.

Miller, E. J. and Gwynne, G. V. (1972) *A Life Apart: A Pilot Study of Residential Institutions for the Physically Handicapped and the Young Chronic Sick*, London: Tavistock.

Mitteis, H. (1975) *The State in the Middle Ages: A Comparative Constitutional History of Feudal Europe*, H. F. Orton (trans.). Oxford: North-Holland.

Morgan, G. (1993) *Imaginization: The Art of Creative Management*. Newbury Park, CA: Sage.

Mugford, S. (1991) Least bad solutions to the 'drugs problem', *Drug and Alcohol Review*, 10, 401–15.

Nettleton, S. (1997) Governing the risky self: How to become healthy, wealthy and wise, in A. Petersen and R. Bunton (eds) *Foucault, Health and Medicine*. London: Routledge.

Nicholls, Sir G. (1854) *A History Of The English Poor Law*, Vol. I. London: John Murray.

Norris, C. (1989) 'Avoiding trouble: the patrol officer's perception of the public', M. Weatheritt (ed.) *Police Research: Some Future Prospects*. Aldershot: Gower.

Nurses, Midwives and Health Visitors Act (1979) 27 and 28 Elizabeth II, CHAPTER 36.

Nursing Homes and Mental Nursing Homes Regulations (1984) Statutory Instruments, 1984, No. 1578. London: HMSO.

Oxford Dictionary (1964) *The Concise Oxford Dictionary of Current English*, 5th edn, revd by E. McIntosh. Oxford: Clarendon Press.

Oxford English Dictionary (1989) *The Oxford English Dictionary*, 2nd edn, prepared by J. A. Simpson and E. S. C. Weiner. Oxford: Clarendon Press.

Øvretveit, J. (1993) *Coordinating Community Care: Multidisciplinary Teams and Care Management*. Buckingham: Open University Press.

Parker, R. (1990) *Safeguarding Standards*. London: National Institute for Social Work.

Parsons, T. (1951) *The Social System*. London: Routledge and Kegan Paul.

Parsons, T. (1964) Introduction, M. Weber, *Theory of Social and Economic Organisation*, T. Parsons and A. M. Henderson (trans.). New York: Free Press.

Parsons, T. (1966) Professions, D. L. Sills (ed.) *International Encyclopedia of the Social Sciences, Vol. 12*. New York: Macmillan; Free Press.

Parton, N. (1985) *The Politics of Child Abuse*. Basingstoke; Macmillan.

Parton, N. (1989) Child abuse, in B. Kahan (ed.) *Child Care Research, Policy and Practice*. London: Hodder and Stoughton.

Parton, N. (1996) Social work, risk and 'the blaming system', in N. Parton (ed.) *Social Theory, Social Change and Social Work*. London: Routledge.

Parton, N. and Parton, C. (1989) Child protection, the law and dangerousness, in O. Stevenson (ed.) *Public Policy and Professional Practice*. Hemel Hempstead: Harvester Wheatsheaf.

Peters, T. (1992a) *Thriving on Chaos: Handbook for the Management Revolution*. London: Pan Books.

Peters, T. (1992b) *Liberation Management: Necessary Disorganization for the Nanosecond Nineties*. London: BCA.

Pidgeon, N., Hood, C., Jones, D., Turner, B. and Gibson, R. (1992) Risk perception, in The Royal Society (ed.) *Risk: Analysis, Perception and Management*, Report of a Royal Society Study Group. London: The Royal Society.

Pollock, F. and Maitland, Sir F. W. (1923) *The History of English Law, Vol 1*, 2nd edn. Cambridge: Cambridge University Press.

Poole, A. L. (1946) Obligations of society in the XII and XIII centuries, Ford Lectures Delivered in the University of Oxford in Michaelmas Term 1944. Oxford: Oxford Clarendon Press.

Prechel, H. and Gupman, A. (1995) Changing economic conditions and their effects on professional autonomy: an analysis of family practitioners and oncologists, *Sociological Forum*, 10, 245–71.

Public Concern at Work (1997) *Abuse in Care: A Necessary Reform*. London: Public Concern at Work.

Race, D. (1995) Historical development of service provision, in N. Malin (ed.) *Services for People with Learning Disabilities*. London: Routledge.

Rapaport, R. N. (1960) *Community as Doctor*. London: Tavistock.

Reder, P., Duncan, S. and Gray, M. (1993) *Beyond Blame: Child Abuse Tragedies Revisited*. London: Routledge.

Registered Homes Act (1984) 32 and 33 Elizabeth II, CHAPTER 23.

Report of the Committee of Enquiry into Mental Handicap Nursing and Care (1979) Chairman, Peggy Jay, Cmnd 7468.1. London: HMSO.

Report of the Committee of Inquiry into Allegations of Ill-Treatment of Patients and other Irregularities at the Ely Hospital Cardiff (1969) Chairman Geoffrey Howe, Cmnd 3975. London: HMSO.

Report of the Committee of Inquiry into Normansfield Hospital (1978) Cmnd 7357. London: HMSO.

Report of the Inquiry into the Care and Treatment of Christopher Clunis (1994) Chairman, J. H. Ritchie. London: HMSO.

Reuter, P. and Caulkins, J. P. (1995) Redefining the goals of national drug policy: recommendations from a working group, *American Journal of Public Health*, 85, 1059–63.

Rhodes, T. (1997) Risk theory in epidemic times: Sex, drugs and the social organisation of 'risk behaviour', *Sociology of Health and Illness*, 19, 208–27.

Riska, E. and Wegar, K. (1995) The medical profession in the Nordic countries; medical uncertainty and gender-based work, in T. Johnson, G. Larkin and M. Saks (eds) *Health Professions and the State in Europe*. London: Routledge.

Ritzer, G. (1993) *The McDonaldization of Society*. Thousand Oaks, CA: Pine Forge Press.

Roethlisberger, F. J. and Dickson, W. J. (1939) *Management and the Worker: An Account of a Research Program Conducted by the Western Electric Company, Hawthorne Works, Chicago*. Cambridge, MA: Harvard University Press.

Rothman, D. (1971) *The Discovery of the Asylum: Social Order and Disorder in the New Republic*. Boston, MA: Little, Brown.

Rousseau, J. J. (1968) *The Social Contract*, M. Cranston (trans and intro.). Harmondsworth: Penguin.

Royal Society, The (1992) *Risk: Analysis, Perception and Management*, Report of a Royal Society Study Group. London: The Royal Society.

St James and Seacroft University Hospitals (1995) *A Guide to Risk Management*. Leeds: St James and Seacroft University Hospitals NHS Trust.

Schön, D. A. (1988) From technical rationality to reflection-in-action, in J. Dowie and A. Elstein (eds) *Professional Judgment: A Reader in Clinical Decision Making*. Cambridge: Cambridge University Press.

Scott, W. (1966) Professionals in bureaucracies, in H. Vollmer and D. Mills (eds) *Professionalization*. Engelwood Cliffs, NJ: Prentice Hall.

Seaton, M. (1997) It's hot in Sweden, *The Observer*, 14 December, 52.

Seebohm, F. (1968) *Report of the Committee on Local Authority and Allied Personal Social Services*, Cmnd. 3703. London: HMSO.

Single, E. (1997) The concept of harm reduction and its application to alcohol: the 6th Dorothy Black Lecture, *Drugs: Education, Prevention, and Policy*, 4, 7–22.

Smith, G. and Cantley, C. (1985) *Assessing Health Care*. Buckingham: Open University Press.

Stanley, N. and Manthorpe, J. (1997) Risk assessment: developing training for professionals in mental health work, *Social Work and Social Sciences Review*, 7 (1), 26–38.

Stimson, G. (1990) AIDS and HIV: the challenge for British drug services, *British Journal of Addiction*, 85, 329–40.

Stimson, G. V. and Thom, B. (1997) Reducing drug- and alcohol-related harm, *Drugs: Education, Prevention, and Policy*, 4, 3–6.

Strang, J. and Farrell, M. (1992) Harm minimisation for drug misusers: when second best may be best first, *British Medical Journal*, 304, 1127–8.

Tait, P. (1996) *Confidential Reporting Systems: The CHIRP Perspective, Confidential Human Factors Incident Reporting Programme*. Bucks: CHIRP.

Tierney, B. (1959) *Medieval Poor Law, A Sketch of Canonical Theory and Its Application in England*. Berkeley and Los Angeles, CA: University of California Press.

Tindale, S. (1998) Procrastination, precaution and the global gamble, in J. Franklin (ed.) *The Politics of Risk Society*. London: Institute for Public Policy Research.

Tindall, L. and Alaszewski, A. (1996) National Policies and the Care of Adults with Learning Disabilities – A Brief Historical Review, Working Paper 11, Risk and Social Welfare Series, Institute of Health Studies. University of Hull.

Tizard, J., Sinclair, I. and Clarke, R. V. G. (1975) *Varieties of Residential Experience*. London: Routledge and Kegan Paul.

Trist, E. L., Higgin, G. W., Murray, H., Pollock, A. B. (1963) *Organizational Choice: Capabilities of Groups at the Coal Face Under Changing Technologies: The Loss, Re-discovery and Transformation of a Work Tradition*. London: Tavistock.

Turner, B. A. (1992) Stepping into the Same River Twice: Learning to Handle Unique Management Problems, Middlesex University Inaugural Lecture, Middlesex University, London.

Turner, B. S. (1994) *Orientalism, Postmodernism and Globalism*. London: Routledge.

Turner, B. S. (1997) Foreword: from governmentality to risk, some reflections on Foucault's contribution to medical sociology, in A. Petersen and R. Bunton (eds) *Foucault, Health and Medicine*. London: Routledge.

United Kingdom Central Council for Nursing, Midwifery and Health Visiting (1992) *Code of Professional Conduct*. London: UKCC.

UKCC (1996) *Guidelines for Professional Practice*. London: United Kingdom Central Council for Nursing, Midwifery and Health Visiting.

Viscusi, W. K. (1992) *Smoking: Making the Risky Decision*. Oxford: Oxford University Press.

Warner, Sir Fredrick (1992) Introduction, in The Royal Society (ed.) *Risk: Analysis, Perception and Management*, Report of a Royal Society Study Group. London: The Royal Society.

Warren, W. L. (1987) *The Governance of Norman and Angevin England 1086–1272*. Stanford, CA: Stanford University Press.

Waugh, S. L. (1988) *The Lordship of England, Royal Wardships and Marriages in English Society and Politics 1217–1327*. Princeton, NJ: Princeton University Press.

Weber, M. (1927) *General Economic History*. New York: Greenberg.

Weber, M. (1947) *The Theory of Social and Economic Organization*, A. M. Henderson and T. Parsons (trans.), T. Parsons (intro.). New York: The Free Press.

Weber, M. (1964) *Theory of Social and Economic Organisation*, T. Parsons and A. M. Henderson (trans.). New York: The Free Press.

Weber, M. (1968a) *Economy and Society, Vol. 1*. New York: Bedminster Press.

Weber, M. (1968b) *Economy and Society, Vol. 3*. New York: Bedminster Press.

Weiss, M. and Fitzpatrick, R. (1997) Challenges to medicine: the case of prescribing, *Sociology of Health and Illness*, 19, 297–327.

Westley, W. A. (1970) *Violence and the Police: a Sociological Study of Law, Custom and Morality*. Cambridge, MA: MIT Press.

Wharton, F. (1992) Risk management: basic concepts and general principles, in J. Ansell and F. Wharton (eds) *Risk: Analysis, Assessment and Management*. Chichester: John Wiley.

Whitaker, P. (1997) I've chosen humanity over rationality, *The Independent*, 18 December 1997.

Wildavsky, A. (1985) *Trial without Error: Anticipation vs Resilience as Strategies for Risk Reduction*. Sydney: Centre for Independent Studies.

Wildavsky, A. (1988) *Searching for Safety*. New Brunswick: Transaction Books.

Williams, B. (1990) *Descartes: The Project of Pure Enquiry*. London: Penguin.

Williams, R. (1994) Hill drives back the shadows, *Independent on Sunday*, 25 September 1994, Sport, 3.

Wolfensberger, W. (1980) A brief overview of the principle of normalization, R. J. Flynn and K. E. Nitsch (eds) *Normalization, Social Integration and Community Services*. Baltimore, MD: University Park Press.

Wright, K., Haycox, A. and Leedham, I. (1994) *Evaluating Community Care: Services for People with Learning Difficulties*. Buckingham: Open University Press.

Yalow, R. S. (1985) Radioactivity in the service of humanity, *Thought*, 60 (236) 517.

Young, A. P. (1994) In the patient's best interests, law and professional conduct, in G. Hunt (ed.) *Ethical Issues in Nursing*. London: Routledge.

Zimmerman, D. and Wieder, D. (1977) The diary-interview method, *Urban Life*, 5 (4): 479–99.

INDEX